Guidance for Incident Management

According to ISO/IEC 20000 & 9001 Standards, Six Sigma and ITSM Best Practices

My eyes established a vision for my life,

After seeing the beauty of Lord Shri Krishna (with belief, devotion and love).

My senses started working intelligently,

After understanding the morals of Lord Shri Krishna's stories and his past times (with belief, devotion and love).

My hands started writing good books,

After folding hands in front of Lord Shri Krishna (with belief, devotion and love).

Oh Lord Krishna, what am I without your blessing?

Oh Lord Krishna, your blessing is the reason for my breath, for my actions, for health, for prosperity, for peace and everything that I possess.

Hare Krishna Hare Krishna, Krishna Krishna Hare Hare,

Hare Rama Hare Rama, Rama Rama Hare Hare,

Dedicated to Swayam Bhagavan Shree Krishna!

Table of contents

Register This Book and Get a Gift!

Thank you very much for purchasing this book.

First of all, before you read ahead, please **register your book** and **get your gift** now:

https://servicemanagers.org/im-registration

As a **ServiceManagers.org IM Book Club** member, you will receive lots of benefits and support from our Book Club:

https://servicemanagers.org/im-book-club

Certification Program

This is the official book for taking the ServiceManagers.Org Certified **Incident Management Professional**™ (**IMP**™) program:

https://servicemanagers.org/incident-management-certification

This Career Program will improve your job opportunities and certify your skills gained from this book.

The Certification Exam is online, and once you sign up you can take it whenever you want (no deadline limits). Just sign up today for your exam, and start enjoying this book.

Preface

Today there are numerous books on ITSM, but none which tells how to implement and improve ITSM practices for organizations, how to bring effectiveness in ITSM operations, and other critical decisions in ITSM operations. Hence, I have chosen to write books on this area while providing detailed information. "Guidance for Incident Management" is the first book of this series with explicit focus on incident management.

This book focuses on niche and essential topics like roles, responsibilities and skills needed in incident management, essentials for incident management operations, implementing incident management through six sigma's DMADV approach, improving incident management through six sigma's DMAIC approach and advice for IM operations.

I should also tell you that this book is not meant for beginners; it is intended only for experienced incident analysts, incident managers, major incident managers, ITSM consultants, service delivery managers, and ITSM process owners. I would say that the prerequisite for reading this book is that the reader should have at least got certified in ITIL Foundation along with some working experience in incident management. This book doesn't focus on the basic and routine topics (which were covered myriad times in numerous other ITSM books).

Next, this book has not been written just for the sake of writing 'beating around the bush' on the same topics with some flowery words and images (and explanations) just to increase the number of pages. The only intention I had while writing this book was to give pragmatic knowledge which I have gained in my experience and knowledge which is not available in any ITSM best practices, standards, ITSM books, and any other ITSM websites.

Finally, if you are not beginner for ITSM and if you would like to gain in-depth knowledge on incident management and efficient operations of IM, then you can buy this book.

Note: This book has been written to give a wealth of knowledge for IM operational staff, IM managers, and ITSM consultants. There are no diagrams/beautification elements in this book; it is just acute knowledge that is not available anywhere.

Acknowledgments

If I have to start thanking people name by name,

I would first thank my mother Krishna Kumari Pabbathi for giving birth to me with all my organs and body in good condition.

I would thank my father Surya Prakash Pabbathi for teaching me the right morals, values, and placing me in one of the best school while sacrificing his comforts and pleasures.

I would thank my grandfather Satyanarayana Pabbathi who iterated that good books are the greatest friends and exemplified his life for principles.

I would thank Balasaraswathi Penmetsa for teaching Mathematics patiently in my 10th grade class, when I was poor at Mathematics, and when no professional teacher could teach me with patience.

I would thank my graduation friend Venkatesham Padigela who inspired me to become a topper in my graduation.

I would thank my friend Subba Rao for helping me and supporting me in many instances of my life.

I would thank my first spiritual alma mater - ISKCON and my first spiritual mentor Kalakanta Prabhu for making me understand life and Lord Krishna (which is best thing that ever happened in all my life).

I know that I am still missing numerous people who have taught, helped, and supported me numerous times in my life.

Hence, I would give my highest respects and would surrender to the Supreme Lord Krishna for arranging all these wonderful people in my life, and for giving me so many lessons, experiences, and knowledge!!!

Big thanks to Angel Berniz, and Servicemanagers.Org for publishing another book of mine.

About the author

Kiran Kumar Pabbathi has worked for various companies in the IT industry which gave him detailed insight of ITSM, ITAM, IAM, Cloud and EAM best practices.

Kiran has had the privilege to work in different roles taking care of service desk operations, request fulfillment, incident management, sharepoint administration, project management, ITIL consulting and trainings, and ITAM consulting.

Kiran is a certified professional in ITIL® Expert, PRINCE2® (Foundation and Practitioner), ISO/IEC 31000 and ISO/IEC 27005 Certified Risk Manager, Six Sigma Green Belt, ISO/IEC20K – Foundation, Cloud Computing – Foundation, TMAP – Foundation (Test Management Professional), MCP in SharePoint 2003 Customizations, and MCTS in MS Project 2007. Kiran is also an accredited ITIL trainer and Invigilator from BCS, UK.

His other works include:

- "PDCA for ITIL – Metrics, CSFs and workflows for implementing ITIL practices" published by TSO, UK (ISBN 9780117082076) which gives a direction for implementing ITIL processes and designing ITSM solutions.
- "Charm of friendship" published by Pothi, India (ISBN 9789382715924) explaining the importance of friendship for children.
- "Guidance for ITAM – Step by step implementation guide with workflows, metrics, best practices and checklists" published by Servicemanagers.org (ISBN 9780991320509)

- "Guidance for EAM (Enterprise Asset Management) – Processes, Implementation steps, workflows, metrics, best practices and checklists" published by Servicemanagers.org (ISBN 9780991320516) which details the guidance for planning, developing and improving EAM processes with KPIs, best practices, workflows and checklists.
- "Focus on IAM (Identity and Access Management) – CSFs, metrics, best practices, checklists and guidelines for defining IAM processes and implementing IAM solutions" published by Servicemanagers.org (ISBN 9780991320530).
- "Guidance for Problem Management - According to ISO/IEC 20000 & 9001 Standards, Six Sigma and ITSM Best Practices" published by Servicemanagers.org, Spain (ISBN 9780991320554)
- "Guidance for Change Management - According to ISO/IEC 20000 & 9001 Standards, Six Sigma and ITSM Best Practices" published by ServiceManagers.Org (ISBN 9780991320561)
- "Focus on Data Center – An IT consultant's essential guide for working in Data Center environment" published by ServiceManagers.Org (ISBN 9780991320578)

15

Introduction to Incident Management

Basic Terminology

Best practices: Practices that are well recognized and which have proved the ability for demonstrating success in respective discipline/industries (e.g. PMBOK for project management, ITIL for IT service management, MOF for IT service management, COBIT for IT governance, etc.).

Cloud application: An application that is hosted on a cloud and accessed via internet.

Cloud Service Provider (CSP): A service provider who offers cloud services or services from a cloud.

Cloud outage: It is the breakdown (unavailability) of cloud services for a period of time.

DFSS/ DMADV: A systematic methodology defined in six sigma philosophy to design products and processes which can meet customer expectations.

DMAIC: A systematic methodology defined in six sigma philosophy for process improvement.

Capability: Any intangible assets like processes, knowledge used in managing an application, IT service or other configuration item (CI).

Critical success factor (CSF): Vital principles necessary for the success of a business; based on CSFs, metrics are developed.

Event: Any occurrence/observation that has significance to the delivery of IT services. Events are notifications that are received through email/mobile devices created by IT service, configuration device, or monitoring tools.

Functional escalation: Informing, involving and seeking the help of different technical teams like availability, capacity, etc. to resolve an incident and restore services.

Hierarchical escalation: Informing, involving, and seeking help from senior levels of management from a specific process or team to assist in escalation.

Hypervisor: It is software that enables one to create, run, and manage virtual machines or instances of an IT resource. Hypervisor actually controls the host processor and its resources and manages to create, and run different virtual instances. Hypervisors is also called virtual machine manager.

Impact: Measure that defines the number of users affected by an outage. Usually denoted as 1,2,3,4.

Incident: Any unplanned breakdown or reduction in the quality of IT service delivered by a service provider is called an incident.

Incident category: A structure that organizes a group of similar types of incidents.

Incident management: Process (in Service Operations) for managing the lifecycle of incidents; it defines a standardized process for registering, categorizing, prioritizing, assignment, diagnosis, escalation, resolution, and closure of an incident.

Incident model: It is a predefined workflow that is followed for regular and routine kind of incidents. It defines a repeatable way of dealing with a particular type of incident.

Incident record: A record that contains the details of the incident. An incident record should have the complete details of the incident from its inception phase to the closure phase.

Infrastructure: Combination of hardware, software, and people-ware in an organization.

ITSM (Information Technology Service Management): Management of IT services to meet the organization's business goals.

Key performance indicator (KPI): Vital metrics necessary for an organization to meet its business goals which reflect the CSFs of an organization.

Major incident: An incident that has a huge impact and urgency to stakeholders and disrupts very critical business services.

Managed private cloud: An approach for cloud management where a third-party organization manages a single client's cloud environment. In this model, a customer provides all the cloud IT equipment and infrastructure, but it is managed by third party human resources. This model is in contrast to multi-tenancy approach in typical clouds.

Mean time between failures (MTBF): Metric that defines the average time that a CI or IT Service can operate its agreed function without any breakdown.

Mean time between system incidents (MTBSI): MTBSI is the mean time from when an IT Service fails, until when it next fails. MTBSI can be derived through the formula, MTBSI = MTBF + MTRS.

Mean time to repair: Average time taken to repair a CI or service after an outage.

Mean time to restore service: Average time taken to restore a CI or service after an outage.

Metric: Measurements that quantitatively evaluate the performance of IT operations.

Policy: Policy is a management directive that significantly influences processes and procedures.

Priority: Measure used to identify the criticality of an incident. Usually denoted as 1, 2, 3, and 4. Calculated through the formula, Priority= (Impact + Urgency)/2.

Process: A set or sequence of activities that results in achieving an output or business goal.

Resources: Any tangible assets (like IT infrastructure, people, money, or anything) that will be helpful to deliver an IT service.

Sigma: It is a Greek letter representing a statistical unit of measurement that defines the standard deviation of a population which measures the variability or spread of the data.

Six Sigma: An approach to improve the process quality by eliminating defects and minimizing variability.

Service: Provision of value to customers without any ownership of risks and internal costs associated in developing a service.

Standard: Rules and conventions that help to implement policies and enforce required conventions.

Urgency: Measure that defines how soon the service has to be restored. Usually denoted as 1,2,3,4.

Objectives of Incident Management

- To define standard process and procedures for managing and resolving incidents in IT infrastructure.
- Resolve the disruptions and restore the services.
- Enhance user satisfaction by restoring IT services as quickly as possible.
- Reduce downtime and provide timely resolution on incidents as per defined agreements.

Objectives of DMAIC and DMADV

- To define effective and efficient processes.
- To improve the consistency and efficiency of processes.
- To improve customer satisfaction and reduce the operational costs.
- To solve issues and reduce variation.

A Day of an Incident and Major Incident Manager

Incident manager

An incident manager's life in an organization would be the most exciting and challenging among all the roles in ITSM. I would say that he probably would be the busiest person throughout all his 8 hours or 9 hours of day.

Once the Incident manager arrives at the office, he would first check if there were any critical incidents in the previous shift. Well by now, you should understand that incident management roles work in shifts (24*7) because incident management main objective is to restore the services as soon as possible. Incidents can occur at any point of time; hence, there is a need for incident manager and incident management staff to work in shifts providing support 24*7.

So, the first incident manager checks his mail box, whether or not there are any critical incidents and priority issues happening; then, he also checks from the other shift incident manager:

If there were any critical incidents which have occurred and gotten closed, he gets all the information about the incident right from the beginning of the closure state. He would get the master ticket and child tickets of that critical incident and would study the complete details to understand what was the issue, who reported it, how was it categorized, what was its impact and priority, who all were involved in the resolution, time taken to resolve the issue, how was it resolved, etc. to be well aware of the IT operations.

If there were any critical incidents which have occurred and the issues are still not resolved, then he would understand the incidents by studying the details of the ticket like what was the issue, who reported it, how was it categorized, what was its impact and priority, its SLA's, etc. Then he would proceed in leading and coordinating with his staff to restore the service as early as possible. Also he is accountable for giving regular and up-to-date information about the incident to the key management.

Once his/her follow up of critical incidents is done, he will do multitasking on different aspects like:

- He will have to get the information on all the critical incidents and also the incidents that are about to breach the SLA's (with respect to response time and resolution time).

- He will have to randomly check the queue to see that the tickets are been picked by the IM staff promptly without missing the response time.

- He will investigate why some incidents are assigned multiple times to different teams playing "pass the buck" game.

- He will have to coordinate with 3rd party vendors to get some issues resolved.

- He will have to check the recurring incidents and log the problem tickets.

- He will have to identify the technology areas where there are no knowledge articles.

- He will have to check the quality of the incident tickets.

- He will have to get involved in CAB meetings, SIP meetings, etc.

At any point of time, if there is any critical incident again, he has get into his shoes and ensure the incident is resolved by coordinating with different stakeholders.

At the end of the day/week, he will be preparing a weekly report about the incidents that has been logged, resolved, breached the SLA's, pending, closed and will send it to the SMO (Service management officer).

Also he will be the responsible person for sending the monthly reports too.

Major incident manager

Once the Major incident manager arrives the office, he would first check if there were any major incidents in the previous shift. Even major incident managers would be working in shifts (24*7) because major incident management is also about restoring the services as soon as possible. Major incidents can occur at any point of time; hence, there is a need of major incident manager to work in shifts providing support 24*7.

So the first incident manager checks whether or not there are any major incidents from the other shift major incident manager.

If there were any major incidents which have occurred and gotten closed, he gets all the information about the major incident right from the beginning to the closure state. He would get the master ticket and child tickets of that major incident and would study the complete details to understand what was the issue, who reported it, how was it categorized, what was its impact and priority, when did the bridge call start, who all were involved in the bridge call, time taken to resolve the issue, how was it resolved, etc. to be well aware of the IT operations.

If there were any major incidents which have occurred and the issue is still not resolved, then he would first understand the incident by studying the details of the ticket like what was the issue, who reported it, how was it categorized, what was its impact and priority, when did the bridge call start (if it already started), etc. Then, he would confirm whether or not he understood the incident correctly (offline), and accordingly he would proceed with coordination with other stakeholders to restore the service as early as possible.

Roles and Responsibilities in Incident management

Incident Manager

Incident Manager manages and coordinates the incident management team and aims at restoring normal service operations while minimizing disruption to business. It also includes proactive identification of trends to minimize the impact of incidents that cannot be prevented.

Responsibilities of Incident Manager

- Manage the incident management team (work of incident support staff), operations, and process end to end requirements.
- Manage high severity incidents and drive their resolution from beginning to end.
- Drive the efficiency and effectiveness of the incident management process.
- Monitor the effectiveness of incident management and make recommendations for improvement.
- Facilitate the restoration of service by getting involved in discussions and identifying resulting action items.
- Ensure that the right skilled (technically knowledgeable) staff is working on incidents.
- Keep the customers and internal stakeholders up to date on high priority incidents through timely and regularly written and verbal communications.
- Review and evaluate reported incidents and formulate a plan of action for handling the incident/issues based on area of expertise/responsibility.
- Reviews with PM team to know the status of workarounds, perm fixes, and RCA's.
- Gets involved in meetings and reviews with the CSI team to help them understand the IM operations.

- Gets involved in meetings with change and release and deployment management teams to understand the new releases.
- Gets involved in meetings with security, availability management and capacity management teams to discuss the security, availability and capacity issues.
- Gets involved in meetings with information security and access management teams to discuss the incidents/issues with respect to security and access issues.
- Monitoring of alerts/tickets and taking the actions necessary to meet SLA targets.
- Ensure incident management process documentation is updated with respect to the change in business requirements.
- Gather and analyze information on a variety of incidents and develop action plans to mitigate and control incidents.
- Implement and comply with the defined incident management process.
- Coordinate incident resolution and ongoing status of all support requests escalated by the organization's service desk.
- Form liaisons with internal training and communications staff to produce user guidance and bulletins explaining best practice and common issues.
- Provide management information and reports on incidents.

Required qualifications and skill set

Technical skills

- Extensive hands-on experience of enterprise and internet IT, networking, deep understanding of virtualization, convergence infrastructure, and different operating systems.

- Familiarity with TCP/IP, network, and storage protocols and procedures.
- Troubleshooting knowledge on performance analysis, HA (High Availability), etc.
- Knowledge of approaches, tools, and techniques for anticipating, recognizing, and resolving technical (hardware, software, application, or operational) problems.
- Knowledge of concepts regarding the design and deployment of information technologies and associated architectural concepts, principles, and tools.
- The ability to define operational and/or technical capacities of servers and networks, and to specify servers and related components needed to meet the high performance requirements and potential growth of various business applications.
- Ability to understand the basic tenets of the physical IT system and that system's relation to the application.
- Experienced in multiple aspects of IT operations, including monitoring and troubleshooting customer response and physical security.

Must have:

- A bachelor's degree in computer science or a related discipline.
- Extensive experience in all aspects of network, virtualization, cloud issues, and stakeholder management.
- Few years of experience in technical support and customer support role.
- Few years of experience in incident management.

- Few years of working experience in cloud computing technologies & services.
- Few technical certifications like CCNA, CCNP, MCSE, etc.
- ITIL v3 or MOF Foundational certification.
- Excellent communication, documentation, and presentation skills.
- Ability to communicate major incident activities across the organization.
- Good analytical and systematic approach to problem solving.
- Excellent judgment, tact, and decision-making ability.
- Understanding of foundational IT technical issues and relationships.

Would be good to have:

- Fundamentals on project management.
- Knowledge on quality assurance and audits.

Incident Analyst

Incident analyst registers, categorizes, prioritizes incidents, and performs investigation to resolve and restore the services.

Responsibilities of Incident analyst

- To provide call support on a rotational basis.
- Analyze, classify, and prioritize incidents.
- Incident investigation and diagnosis (including resolution where possible).
- Coordinating and driving technical incident resolution with operations, service engineering, and development teams.
- Rerouting misdirected incidents that have not been handled in a timely manner.
- Identifying incidents that need special attention or escalation.
- Ensure incident report is created immediately after resolution.
- Real time & continuous follow-ups with global support teams for incident resolution.
- Interface with internal/external customers on operational issues by dispatching on-call engineers, facilitating communication, and driving resolution to events via standard operating procedures.
- Assist others with identifying the impact of incidents.
- Monitoring incident details, including the configuration items affected.
- Detection of possible problems and assignment of problems to the problem management team for them to raise problem records.

- The resolution and recovery of assigned incidents.
- Participation in audit activities related to the incident management process.
- Monitoring the status and progress towards resolution of assigned incidents.
- Keeping affected business partners informed about progress.
- Taking ownership of escalations and escalating as necessary per established escalation policies.

Required qualifications and skill set

Technical skills:

- ITIL v3 Foundation certification.
- Troubleshooting knowledge on desktops, laptops, networking, applications, databases, etc.
- Working knowledge on multiples operating systems like windows, unix, linux, etc.
- Understanding on TCP/IP network environment.

Must have:

- A bachelor's degree in computer science or a related discipline.
- Good written and verbal skills.
- Experience in the use of MS Office products.
- Experience in working with remote teams across multiple time zones.
- Attitude to work in a complex IT environment.
- Ability to prioritize a busy workload.

Major Incident Manager

Major incident manager manages all major incidents to successful resolution; he is accountable as a single source for delivering clear and accurate communications during the major incident's lifecycle to all senior and executive management levels.

Responsibilities of Incident manager

- Responsible for the creation and communication of agreed action plans.
- Communicate/escalate all high priority incidents ensuring that the communication process is adhering to IM process.
- Assist the problem management team to ensure root causes are identified.
- Ensure all agreed operational policies and procedures are adhered to whilst being a champion of the incident management policy process and procedures.
- Responsible for driving troubleshooting and recovery with confidence and authority reducing time to repair on major and crisis outages.
- Contribute to improvement plans on a regular basis; contributing ideas and supporting any identified improvement initiatives ensuring that contributions are documented and progressed.

Required qualifications and skill set

Technical skills:

- ServiceManagers.org Certified Professional in Incident Management (CPIM).
- ISO/IEC 20000 International Standard knowledge.
- QHSE certification.
- Six sigma black belt certification.
- Knowledge in performing RCA (Root cause analysis).
- Troubleshooting experience in databases, operating systems, and applications.
- Troubleshooting knowledge on network environment.
- Experience in system monitoring.

Must have:

- A bachelor's degree in computer science or a related discipline.
- Excellent written and verbal skills.
- Excellent customer relation skills with experience in working with remote teams across multiple time zones and ability to prioritize a busy workload.
- Attitude to work in a complex IT environment on a 24/7 shift schedule (including nights, weekends and holidays).
- Experience in crisis management.
- Experience of managing major incidents affecting critical IT systems and services.
- Excellent communication with experience of a global organization.
- Knowledge and understanding of enterprise IT systems.
- Good communication skills, and customer and service orientation.
- Responsiveness, flexibility and teamwork skills.

Essentials for Incident Management Operations

Kiran Kumar Pabbathi

Process Flow for Incident Management

Process flow for incident management defines a sequence of activities that will result in effective incident management operations aiming at quicker resolution of issues or outages.

Generally in an IT organization, incidents can be detected and raised by end user/ customer, service desk staff, incident management team, 3rd party vendor who is a stakeholder of the IT project, and operations team.

End User: Is the user who is actually using the IT services.

Customer: Is the person or a team who is paying the money for the receiving IT services.

Service Desk Staff: Single point of contact for addressing the issues of users and customers.

L2/L3 team: Point of contact for resolving the issues as per the defined SLA's.

3rdParty Vendor: Another company who is associated with an IT service provider to deliver IT services to the customer.

Operations Team: A team of the IT service provider, who are involved in monitoring kind of activities.

Process Flow - Incident Resolution by L1

Activity 1:

41

Service desk/Incident management detects the incident from the user or customer through phone call/email/chat interaction.

Activity 2:

Service desk/Incident management team verifies if the caller or requester is an authorized user and categorizes whether or not the issue is an incident/service request.

Activity 3:

If its determined as an incident, then more details regarding the incident is gathered.

Activity 4:

Service desk/ Incident management team checks whether or not it's a new incident or already logged incident.

Activity 5:

Accordingly, an incident ticket is raised in the service management tool, with complete description, impact, urgency, etc.

Activity 6:

Service desk/Incident management team checks its knowledge base and tries to resolve the issue if it's in their scope. If it's not in their scope, then the ticket is assigned to L2/L3 team.

Activity 7:

After troubleshooting and if the issue is resolved, then the ticket is resolved.

Activity 8:

After setting the incident ticket in resolved status and after 3 days of time, then the ticket is closed.

Note: If the user/customer has any issue with the resolved ticket, then the ticket is reopened.

Process Flow - Incident Resolution by L2/ L3

Service desk/Incident management team checks its knowledge base and tries to resolve the issue if it's not in their scope, then the ticket is assigned to L2/L3 team.

Activity 1:

L2 team verifies if the troubleshooting is done on the correct CI.

Activity 2:

L2 team checks if it's a critical or major incident. If it's a major incident, it is assigned to major incident team.

Activity 3:

L2 team gathers complete information about the CI using the CMDB and historical incidents.

Activity 4:

If L2/L3 team is not able to resolve the issue, then they contact the vendor.

Activity 5:

A 3rd part company or vendor is involved and their help is taken to resolve the issue.

Activity 6:

Once the issue is resolved, the troubleshooting steps performed by the 3rd party company are documented and sent as knowledge articles for the knowledge manager to publish it as a knowledge article.

Activity 7:

After setting the incident ticket in resolved status and after 3 days of time, then the ticket is closed.

Activity 8:

After setting the incident ticket in resolved status and after 3 days of time, then the ticket is closed.

Note: If the user/customer has any issue with the resolved ticket, then the ticket is reopened.

Process Flow for Major Incident Management

Process flow for major incident management defines a sequence of activities that will result in effective major incident management operations aiming at quicker resolution of issues or outages.

Generally, in an IT organization, major incidents are created by the incident management team after carefully understanding the issue.

Process Flow – Major Incident Resolution

Activity 1:

Major incident management team receives an alert about a major incident.

Activity 2:

Major incident management team consolidates all information about the incident and determines whether or not it's a major incident.

Activity 3:

If it's determined that it's a major incident, Major incident management team communicates it to the customer management and the relevant stakeholders through email.

Activity 4:

Major incident management team opens the bridge call, inviting all the relevant technical SME's and the 3rd party company of the CI (if necessary).

Activity 5:

Once the issue is resolved, the bridge call is closed and informed to all the stakeholders and customer management that the issue has been resolved.

Activity 6:

Accordingly, a problem ticket is also raised to understand the RCA and to identify the permanent fix.

Activity 7:

Once the end user is satisfied, document all the troubleshooting steps and send it to knowledge manager for publishing in a knowledge article.

Activity 8:

A review meeting is conducted on the major incident like a PIR to understand what went well and what went wrong. Accordingly, lessons learned are shared with the stakeholders.

Metrics for IM operations

Metrics for IM operations are essential ingredients that assess and evaluate the performance of operational activities and will stand as basis for improvement.

Metrics for IM operations can be mentioned as below:

- Total number of incidents logged in a month
- Number of incidents resolved by the level 1 analysts
- Number of incidents resolved by the level 2 analysts
- Number of first time fixes
- Number of incidents that are incorrectly assigned
- Number of incidents that are incorrectly prioritized
- Number of incidents that are incorrectly categorized
- Number of recurring incidents
- Number of incidents that needed onsite human resources intervention
- Number of incident records created in the IMIS
- Number of major incidents
- Number of minor incidents
- Number of normal incidents
- Number of incidents categorized as problems
- Number of incidents that were resolved by third party companies
- Number of incidents that were functionally escalated
- Number of incidents that were hierarchically escalated
- Number of incidents that are closed and reopened
- Number of incidents that breached SLAs
- Number of incidents handled by incident models
- Size of incident backlog
- CSAT rating on incident resolution

47

- Mean time to restore services (MTRS) for major incidents
- Mean time to restore services (MTRS) for normal incidents
- Mean time between system incidents (MTBSI)
- Mean time between failures (MTBF)
- Average cost associated with major incidents
- Average cost associated with normal incidents
- Adherence to process defined
- IM staff utilization rate

Metrics for IM process

Metrics for IM process are essential ingredients that assess and evaluate the defined process and its implementation, and it will stand as basis for improvement.

Metrics for IM process can be mentioned as below:

- Time taken to develop IM process and its collaterals
- Number of resources and man days required for process development
- Number of resources and man days required for process testing
- Number of resources and man days required for process collaterals editing
- Number of technical discrepancies found in all process collaterals
- Number of linguistic discrepancies (typos, confusions, grammatical errors) found in process documentation
- Number of defects found by end users and customer teams
- Number of documentation deliverables (process guides, standard operating procedures, work instructions, role & responsibilities) available on a process
- Number of NC's (Non-conformances) found in audits with respect to process
- Number of areas where there is no documentation available
- Number of operational activities which are not addressed by the defined process

- Number of process training sessions provided in a year/ half a year
- Customer satisfaction rating on process documentation provided
- Customer satisfaction rating on process training sessions and trainer

Best Practices

Best practices are those real practices that have delivered efficient, effective, and excellent results in the IT processes and real operations.

Best practices for IM processes and operations can be defined as mentioned below:

- **Detect incidents as early as possible**

  Management can deploy some good event monitoring tools to detect events and take appropriate action preventing incidents with huge impact.

- **Incident manager should not be engaged only as an escalation point or for escalations**

  It is a very common bad practice in organizations that incident managers are only used as escalation points, for managing escalations, or for doing follow ups. Incident managers should also be involved in diagnosis and resolution which will enable the team to provide quicker solutions.

- **Maintenance of incidents records for all incidents**

  All incidents information throughout the lifecycle should be captured and documented with complete information which will be helpful for future references to operational and management staff.

- **Define control procedures for managing incident tickets**

  Definition of control procedures for managing incident tickets should be like:

  1. Closed incident ticket cannot be reopened, unless

51

there is a business justification.
2.   Priority of an incident ticket cannot be increased/
reduced, unless there is a business justification.
3.   Incidents cannot be closed without end user's
consent.

- **Definition of incident models for routine issues**
Incident models define pre-defined steps for handling
particular types of incidents that are routine, and these
models can save great time and effort for the IM staff
without reinventing the wheel.

- **Thorough understanding of SLAs, OLAs and UCs**
Unawareness on the SLAs, OLAs, and UCs causes most of
the penalizations and SLA breaches. Hence,
management should make a conscious effort to make
adequate awareness of SLAs, OLAs, and UCs for all
services through training, posters, etc.

- **Access to KEDB, CMDB, CMS and SKMS**
IM staff should have access to KEDB, CMDB, CMS and
SKMS; accessibility to these tools will help the IM staff to
understand the impact of incident, associated services
with the incident, SLAs associated, financial value, etc.
and will help them to restore the services quickly.

- **Organized KEDB and KB**
KEDB and KB will be accessed continuously by every IM
staff in day to day operations; hence, the incident
manager should take a meticulous effort in checking the
quality of the KEDB and KB. Organized KEDB and KB's
means:

- Every article should be identified with a unique registration number
- Every article should have a brief description
- Every article should be associated with a keyword
- Every article should have been approved and
  - tested by the respective process owner and operational manager
- Articles should be categorized based on the topic
- Frequently occurring issues should be easily accessible
- Every article should mention the date when it was created
- Every article should have the rating feature to record satisfaction/feedback on the article provided.

- **Conducting meetings with incident management team**
  Incident manager should have daily meetings with IM staff discussing:
  - the P1, P2, P3, and P4 issues logged for the day
  - the incidents which are about breach the SLAs
  - the incidents which were reopened again
  - the incidents which received low CSat
  - the incidents that received very good CSat

- **Maintenance of ITSM process owners and onsite technicians contacts list**
  Up to date maintenance of ITSM process owners, onsite technicians, and service owner's contacts details, is a must. This will enable the IM staff to get in touch with the right person to restore services in the defined SLAs and also get important information about services.

53

CSFs

CSFs (Critical Success Factors) are those foundational pillars that are derived from the vision and mission statement of the organization/department; these factors will help operational managers/process owners in establishing or developing the necessary IT processes, policies, and executing operations.

- **Selection of right human resources**
  Selection of right human resources with great technical knowledge, communication skills, and customer service attitude is a must for IM staff; it can be ranked as a number 1 issue among all the best practices in IM.

- **Define an explicit team for MIM**
  The major incident manager should not be the same person as the Incident manager. There should be an explicit role to handle major incidents with special and different procedures to restore services.

- **Regular process and technology training for IM staff**
  Training on IM process, policies, procedures, and technical knowledge is a must which should happen at regular intervals.
  Most of the delays and discrepancies in IM operations happen due to unawareness on IM process, policies, and procedures; hence, it is a mandatory objective for IT management to conduct training which can bring thorough awareness to all stakeholders. Management should also conduct exams and assessments to evaluate

the proficiency of the staff and reward them with some gifts or incentives.

- **Participation of IM staff in service improvement meetings**
  Participation of IM staff in service improvement meetings is very vital to understand the priorities of IT organization and improve the IM process as per the IT goals. Also IM staff can provide many great inputs for improving the IT service delivery.

- **Regular meetings with other ITSM stakeholders**
  Regular meetings with other ITSM process owners and operational managers should happen continuously to understand the trends and patterns of incidents and will also enable the IM staff to understand the root causes of incidents.

- **Integrated ITSM tool that can accommodate all ITSM process activities and functions**
  Management should select and deploy an integrated ITSM tool which can accommodate all ITSM processes and functions; having separate tools for different processes will increase burden (in terms of human resources efforts) and complexity (in terms of technology to do explicit integration).

- **Selection of right ITSM tool**
  Select the right ITSM tool that can fit your business requirements, which can be a single point of contact for all your ITSM processes in your organization, which follows the ITSM terminology and best practices, which has

55

decision making, reporting and data mining capabilities, and which is easy to use.

- **Definition of Incident Management Information System (IMIS)**

  Incident management information system is a repository which stores all incidents records (which encapsulates all incidents information), IM models, IM processes (major, normal and minor), plans and procedures in one place. It enables the key stakeholders like IM process owner, other ITSM process owners, incident manager, and IT service owner to make effective decisions about the IT operations with respect to incident management. Though ITILv3 doesn't mention anything about IMIS, this artifact can be very helpful for getting all information on incident management. Definition of IMIS should be based on appropriate web, reporting, and database technologies which can provide powerful visualization and mapping tools and reporting facilities.

- **Documentation of lessons learned**

  Documentation of lessons learned should be a must, and it should be submitted as knowledge articles for verification, validation, and publication in a knowledge base.

56

Provision of channels to IM tools and ITSM databases

Incident management tools and event management tools and databases

Provision of channels to event management tools and databases with incident management tools would help the IM staff to:

- *Gather more detailed information about an incident through the events triggered by the CIs/services.*

And will help them to make quicker and effective decisions to restore the services quickly.

Incident management tools and service desk tools and databases

Provision of channels to SD tools and databases with incident management tools would help the IM staff to:

- *Gather more detailed information about an incident in customer's voice.*

Provisioning channels to SD tools and databases is not so important and critical; hence, it can be mentioned as an optional requirement.

Incident management tools and problem management databases

Provision of channels to KEDB and problem management databases with incident management tools would help the IM staff to:

- *Identify the temporary fixes developed.*
- *Identify the permanent fixes developed.*

And it will help them to make quicker and effective decisions to restore services quickly.

Incident management and Change management

Provision of channels to change management databases with incident management tools would help the IM staff to:

- *Identify and understand if the outage was caused by any new change that was deployed.*

And it will help them to make quicker and effective decisions to carry out IM operations.

Incident management tools and Service asset and configuration management databases

Provision of channels to CMDB's, CMS's with incident management tools would help the IM staff to:

- *Identify and understand the underlying CIs and internal services associated with a service.*
- *Identify the impact of the incident.*
- *Identify the SLAs associated with a specific service.*

And it will help them to make quicker and effective decisions to carry out IM operations.

Incident management and Release and deployment management

Provision of channels to release management databases with incident management tools would help the IM staff to:

- *Identify and understand if the outage was caused by any new release deployment.*
- *Understand the details and documentation on the new releases, provided by RDM.*

And it will help them to make quicker and effective decisions to carry out IM operations.

Incident management and Availability management

Provision of channels to availability management databases with incident management tools would help the IM staff to:

- *Identify and understand if the outage was caused due to availability issues and will enable them to get in touch with availability management staff to provide resolution.*

Incident management and Capacity management

Provision of channels to capacity management databases with incident management tools would help the IM staff to:

- *Identify and understand if the outage was caused due to capacity issues and will enable them to get in touch with capacity management staff to provide quicker resolutions.*

Incident management and Financial management

Provision of channels to financial management databases with incident management is unnecessary, as it might become a risk.

Note: You can have provide channels/access for Incident managers and Major Incident managers to financial management databases.

Incident management and Service level management

Provision of channels to SLM databases with incident management tools would help the IM staff to:

- *Identify and understand the SLAs, OLAs and UCs associated with a service.*

And will help them to make quicker and effective decisions to carry out IM operations.

Incident management and Continual Service Improvement

Provision of channels to CSI databases with incident management tools would enable the IM staff to:

- *Document new recommendations to improve the services.*
- *Identify improvement opportunities with respect to the trends in IM operations.*

Escalation matrix

Escalation matrix is a documentation which gives information about the points of contacts, email id's, and their contact numbers with respect to different services offered by the service provider.

The purpose of preparing this document is to elucidate the right people/responsible people with respect to different IT services, and accordingly these people will be informed/ consulted about any critical issues in the IT infrastructure.

An example for escalation matrix template can be depicted as mentioned below:

Escalation matrix for storage services

Category	Contact name	Phone number	Email id	Timings (if any)
Service Provider	ABC (1st level contact)	123456789	abc@demo.com	24x7
Service Provider	DEF (2nd level contact)	987654321	def@demo.com	24x7
Service Provider	GHI (3rd level contact)	567891234	ghi@demo.com	9am-5pm
Customer	JKL (1st level contact)	567891234	jkl@cust.com	9am-5pm

Customer	MNO (2nd level contact)	567891234	mno@cust.com	9am-5pm
3rd party company	PQR (1st level contact)	567891234	pqr@3rdpart.com	9am-5pm
3rd party company	STU (2nd level contact)	567891234	stu@3rdpart.com	9am-5pm

Assignment of incident tickets

Assignment groups are the different teams/groups to whom an incident ticket can be assigned so that the appropriate person/SME can look into the issue and fix it.

It's been observed that many incident management teams and even service desk teams do not understand the importance of assignment, resulting in breaches.

- Some incident analysts/service desk analysts do the wrong assignment in ignorance and lack of knowledge; they delay the incident investigation and resolution.

- Some incident analysts/service desk analysts do the wrong assignment involuntarily like typos or some hasty work; and delay the incident investigation and resolution.

Either they do it in involuntarily or because of lack of knowledge; regardless, it's going to impact the MTRS and causes SLA breaches or customer dissatisfaction.

Hence, assignment is a very important and a meticulous task which should be paid a great deal of attention while escalating/assigning it to another team.

Hence, management should educate the importance of assignment/assigning tickets to the right teams/people; it should equip the analysts with clear instructions when an incident should be escalated to vendor support, when it should be functionally escalated, and when it should be hierarchically escalated with some reference guides.

Incident management operations staff should be equipped with a cheat sheet giving information on all assignment groups and criteria for assigning (when the incident should be assigned).

For example:

Service	Criteria	Assignment group
SAP	Errors; Slow performance	SAP administration
Network	Slow performance/ Unavailability issues	Network administration
SAN (Storage Area Network)	Errors	SAN administration

Quality checks on IM tickets

Quality checks on IM tickets is an essential activity performed to ensure that all incidents reported by the end users and stakeholders have been properly registered, classified, categorized, prioritized, diagnosed, resolved, and adequately documented in adherence to the defined process.

Objectives:

- To ensure every IM ticket is handled in the right way (as per defined processes and policies) while focusing on timely resolution (without wrong assignments and ticket hopping)

- To record and track all incidents information (right from the inception to resolution and closure) and the actions performed by IM staff

- To ensure the defined process and process controls are followed

Approach for performing quality checks on IM tickets

Approach for performing quality checks on IM tickets can be explained by the below sequential steps:

- Schedule a meeting with the incident manager and explain the purpose of the quality check on IM tickets. And accordingly, the incident manager has to assign an IM staff member to walk through the sample of IM tickets to the assessor.

- Access the IM tool and get the dump of incident tickets for a specific time period (between dates AA-BB-2013 to DD-XX-2014).

- Select few incidents randomly based on different categories and statuses of incidents like: major incidents, P1 incidents that were resolved and closed, P1 incidents that were assigned to third party company, P1 incidents that are in assigned status, P1 incidents that were closed and reopened, P1 incidents that were closed and received negative Csat, P1 incidents that are in Pending status, and likewise for P2, P3, and P4 incidents.

- Ask the assessee to explain the incidents that were created on the above mentioned criteria.

- Check if the major incidents tickets are documented as per the guidelines.

- Check if the major incident tickets are updated with status update notifications sent to the stakeholders.

- Check if the incident tickets are documented with complete details like:
    o Sequence of events that lead to the incident
    o Sequence of events following the incident

- Check if the incident tickets are being classified appropriately.

- Check if the incident tickets are being assigned to the correct assignment groups based on the guidelines.

- Check if the incident tickets are being prioritized appropriately as per the guidelines.

- Check if the incident tickets are resolved providing complete resolution steps to an incident.

- Check if the incident tickets assigned to third-party companies are following the guidelines.

- Check if the incident tickets are being escalated (functionally/hierarchically) for the right reasons as per the escalation guidelines.

- Check the reasons for ticket hopping from one team to other.

- Check why incidents are breaching SLAs.

- Document all the observations, good practices, bad practices, improvement areas and present a report to the incident manager.

Approach for assessing incident management

IM assessment is an activity performed by an assessor to identify the strengths, weakness, and opportunities in the IM processes and operations which is done by conducting analysis on the process, questionnaires, surveys, and observation in live operations. IM assessment is an essential activity performed on IM process and operations to understand:

- If the process is complete (addressing all the scope of work), effective, and efficient (without redundant and vague activities).

- If the operational teams and its activities are in adherence to the defined process activities.

Approach for IM assessment

Approach for IM assessment can be defined through the below mentioned steps:

- Schedule a meeting with the incident manager and explain the purpose of the IM assessment (Accordingly incident manager has to assign a few IM staff members [like L1 analysts, L2 analysts, Major incident manager, including Incident manager]).

- Analyze the process documents to identify if there are any ambiguities and discrepancies with respect to sequence of actions.

- Analyze if the designed process is robust and complete covering all the scope of work as per the statement of work/SLAs/contracts signed with the customer.

- Analyze if the RACI matrix is defined correctly regarding who is responsible, accountable, consulted, and informed about IM operations to ensure that there is demarcation of roles and responsibilities.

- Analyze if the metrics are aligning to the business goals.

- Check if the process collaterals provide guidelines on escalation, assignment, priority calculation, resolution, and closure of the incident.

- Check if there are defined standard operating procedures (SOP) for all operational activities.

- Conduct interviews with operational staff to evaluate the awareness on IM process and terminology.

- Conduct surveys on the live IM operational activities while operational teams are working on incident tickets and resolving incidents.

- Conduct surveys on the IM operational staff to check if they are following the process, policies, etc.

Checklists for incident management operations staff

Checklists for incident management operations staff will be helpful to IM operational staff to track the complete details of an incident. These details will be very helpful for IM operational staff to understand and diagnose, and they will enable them to provide a quicker resolution.

- Who raised the incident? Where did the incident occur?
- Who are affected by the incident? How many business processes/departments, IT services, and customers are affected?
- How many VIP customers will be affected?
- What is the financial value associated with an incident?
- How many users will be affected approximately?
- What is the associated SLA/timelines to recover from the incident?
- Who owns the IT service and where the incident occurred?
- Are there any incidents logged on the same issue in the past 1-2 days?
- Were there any changes/releases implemented on the service associated with the incident?
- Are there any incidents logged on the same issue in the past few months?
    - How was/were they solved?
    - What was the priority of that incident?
    - Also what was the impact and urgency?
    - Who resolved that incident?
    - Was there an incident record created?
    - Was it resolved in the defined SLA?

- Does this issue need any escalation like functional/hierarchical escalation?
- Is this a major incident? Does it meet the major incident criteria and conditions as defined in the process?
- Is this a known error? Do we have a temp fix in KEDB?
- Do we have a perm fix for the incident?
- Should the incident manager/major incident manager be informed of the incident so that problem management should also be involved?
- Should it be resolved by a third party company? Does it meet the criteria and conditions as defined in the OLAs?

Assessment checklist for incident management operations

Assessment checklist for IM operations will be helpful for IM operational staff to understand how effectively the process has been defined. This checklist can also be used by a quality team to evaluate the effectiveness of process and operations. This assessment checklist can be mentioned as below:

- Do you have defined goals and objectives for incident management, and is the IM staff aware of the goals and objectives?
- Do you have defined scope for incident management process, and is the IM staff aware of it?
- Does your management and operational staff understand the value of incident management to the business?
- Do you have defined Policies, Principles, and Procedures for incident management?
- Do you have defined timescales for all incident handling stages with respect to different incident models?
- Do you have defined incident models for different services?
- Do you create incident records for all major incidents?
- Is there a definition for major incidents and incidents published?
- Is there a definition of triggers, inputs, outputs, and interfaces made for IM process?
- Do you have defined CSFs, KPIs, and metrics?
- Have you tracked the challenges and risks for IM, and do you monitor them regularly?

- Do you get enough training on process and technology to keep your IM staff's knowledge updated?
- Do you have a well-defined knowledge base, KEDB, and IMIS? Do you find any errors or discrepancies in the knowledge articles (in these databases)?
- Can you relate your incident records with the problem records in the ITSM tool?
- Does your IM staff have access to CMS and CMDB's?
- Do you conduct any assessments or evaluation methods to check the knowledge of IM staff?
- Are your incidents and their statuses reported timely and effectively?
- Is the incident handling, processing, and resolution time in line with overall service levels and objectives?
- Are all your incidents managed and stored in a single management system?
- Do you perform major incident reviews after resolving and restoring the major incident?
- Do you have a defined auditing mechanism on all incident records to ensure that all the details are entered and categorized correctly?

Gamification in IM operations

Gamification is a new concept which applies game mechanics and techniques at workplace to motivate people towards better performance, to provide more transparency in awarding and rewarding people, and to provide some fun at work while working and achieving the business objectives of the organization.

This concept is spreading very rapidly in IT industry, and it can drive great benefits to incident management operations as well.

Gamification in IM operations is a fresh approach to bring more interest in work and to provide more transparency among the staff with respect to rewards, hikes in salary, promotions, etc. Gamification in IM operations would mean that all IM operational staff like level 1 analysts, level 2 analysts, and level 3 analysts would strive to gain the maximum number of points/scores by:

- resolving the maximum number of incidents
- resolving the incidents quickly
- identifying new solutions for technical issues
- working more number of hours/weekends/holidays
- getting perfect Csat scores from customer surveys
- giving training sessions
- acting as a mentor
- maintaining quality in IM tickets, etc.

Gamification in IM tools

Gamification in IM tools can also be implemented by defining scores/ points; every IM operators, (who resolve and manage the incidents) who takes the roles like incident manager, major incident manager and incident analysts will be scored in the ITSM tool based on:

- Number of incidents resolved within the SLA
- Number of incidents resolved in a month
- Csat obtained on an incident

And also negative scores can also be assigned to operators who have:

- Incorrectly assigned the tickets
- Not resolved the incidents as per SLAs

So each and every condition mentioned above would have specific scores, and the staff who earns the maximum number of points/scores can be rewarded with gifts/vouchers/cash/etc. Not only that, the employee with the maximum number of scores can also be awarded with the highest hike in salary or can be promoted to a better designation, etc.

Hence this approach can be very beneficial in IM operations to give some fun, competition, confidence, and trust in appraisal system. And for organizations, it would help them to achieve business objectives.

Important details to be captured in IM tickets and reports

Important details to be captured in IM tickets and IM reports are:

- **Incident triggered by:** The source which triggered the incident like email, phone call, etc.
- **Incident number:** Unique ID generated for incident
- **Incident description:** Description of the incident
- **Incident location:** Location where the incident occurred
- **Affected services:** Services affected by the incident
- **Incident triggered by:** CI/CIs which caused the incident
- **Affected CIs:** CIs affected by the incident
- **Event ID:** Event ID (with respect to the incident) that was generated before the incident occurred
- **Incident analyst:** Analyst who did the analysis, categorization, prioritization, and initial diagnosis.
- **Incident reported by:** Person name and contact details who reported the incident
- **Incident date:** Date on which the incident occurred
- **Assignment group:** The group to which the incident has been assigned
- **Impact:** Number of people affected by the incident
- **Urgency:** How soon the incident has to be restored
- **Priority:** It will be based on impact and urgency
- **SLAs associated:** SLAs associated with incident management
- **SLA target date and time:** Date and time when the SLAs will be breached with respect to the incident
- **Third party involved:** Defines if there are any third party companies involved in fixing the incident
- **Category:** Category of the incident (Check the CTI structure mentioned in this book)
- **Type:** Type of the incident (Check the CTI structure mentioned in this book)
- **Item:** Item of the incident (Check the CTI structure mentioned in this book)
- **Major incident review:** Determines if it's an major incident
- **Major incident justification:** Defines the business justification to be called as major incident

- **Escalation:** Defines what type of escalation was needed (hierarchical or functional)
- **Escalation justification:** What is the business justification for escalation?
- **Escalated to:** Name of the person/SME to whom the incident was escalated
- **Associated problems:** Should identify if there are any problem tickets associated with respect to the incident
- **Incident resolved by:** Name of the person who resolved the incident
- **Incident resolved time:** The time when the incident got resolved
- **Incident closed time:** The time when the incident got closed
- Resolution steps: Description of the solution provided as resolution
- **Cause of the incident:** Description on the cause of the incident detailing why and how the incident happened
- **SLAs breach details:** Description of why the SLAs were breached - by how many minutes or hours did we breach the SLAs?
- **Number of incidents on this service:** Defines the number of incidents that occurred on a specific service
- **Outage duration:** Duration of the outage
- **PIR:** Post implementation review details of the incident
- **Csat:** Customer satisfaction on the incident

Preventing and foreseeing incidents

Every IT organization's aim is to avoid and foresee incidents before they affect IT operations. Foreseeing and preventing incidents is very much possible by:

Deploying monitoring tools/event management tools

Deploying monitoring tools/event management tools can be very helpful to foresee the incidents and will also provide a chance to avoid incidents on IT stakeholders and continuity of IT services.

Functionality of these monitoring/event management tools is based on using active/passive polling methods where the server system deploys some rules/criteria for all kinds of abnormal and unusual behavior on client systems in the infrastructure; there will be an administrator monitoring the server system while the console receives notifications. So when there is any abnormal behavior of client systems, a notification or message is sent to the server system and the administrators will act intuitively to rectify the issue by running automated scripts or onsite/manual repairs.

Proactive problem management

Proactive problem management can be very helpful to avoid incidents and problems in IT operations as a proactive PM carries out its activities by analyzing the trends and patterns of past incidents and events generated by IT services and CIs (to understand the root cause, to understand the threats and vulnerabilities). Accordingly, a proactive PM will understand the issues and incidents that can occur on IT services, and it would also define mitigation measures to avoid the incidents.

Active role of CSI

Active role of CSI (Continual Service Improvement) activities and initiatives will bring great advantage for foreseeing incidents, avoiding incidents, and reducing the impact of incidents.

As CSI works with all ITSM processes and functions, it collects improvement initiatives, defects, non-compliance issues, concerns, and recommendations from different process owners, service owners, operational staff, and also end users.

If the CSI team works efficiently by implementing all improvement initiatives, or rectifying all defects, non-compliance issues, concerns, and recommendations on time, the number of incidents will be definitely reduced to a great extent.

Major incident

I have observed that many ITSM working professionals have great confusion and misunderstanding on the term "major incidents" (because they have worked with some organizations where the customer wants all P1 incidents to be called "major incidents" as per their requirements and as per the signed SLA). Therefore, the ITSM professionals have a misconception that all P1 incidents are major incidents.

Hence, here is my approach to bring more clarity on the concept "major incident", and this can be defined as: *Any incident that occurs due to a natural disaster, human error, or a human attack and which disrupts most of the IT services (as a complete failure) impacting huge number of users, creating huge financial losses, and affecting CBFs (Critical Business Function) in working hours.*

Note: Sometimes there would be incidents which has great impact and financial value, but is easily addressed at the helpdesk level as it doesn't involve great complexity. So these kinds of incidents cannot be called as major incidents.

Major incidents generally require special arrangements or should have separate procedures to resolve and restore major incidents. Generally, problem management staff and technical management can also be involved in investigating, diagnosis, and resolution of major incidents.

Note: A service provider should clearly discuss the conditions for a major incident, and should define an effective approach to resolve and restore the issue with respect to the customer's requirements.

Declaration of a major incident can be determined by the intensity of an incident which can be derived by the below mentioned formula; the calculated value should be greater than 0.5.

Intensity of an incident = {Number of IT services failed due to an incident (representing complete failure of IT services)} / Total number of IT services provided by the service provider.

For example:

If a service provider is providing 5 services, like database maintenance and administration, network management, storage service (backup, recovery and archival), communication, and print service in an organization, and assuming there has been an incident where 3 services (network management, storage service, communication) are completely down due to an incident in the productive or working hours of the customer (with respect to the formula mentioned above), the value is equal to 0.6. And since the intensity of the incident is greater than 0.5, this incident can be treated as a major incident.

Note: But this formula cannot be made as a benchmark in all instances (for all types of incidents). As sometimes there might be just a single incident impacting a single service, but which has great financial value.

Essentials for major incident management

* Customer focused approach and methodology
* A separate team for major incidents with clear roles and responsibilities

- Defined SLAs with the service provider; OLAs with internal departments and UCs with 3rd party companies
- Defined templates for critical outage notifications, PIRs, minutes of the meeting (MOM),
- Clearly defined scope mentioning what all services are VBFs, and when a failure should be called as a major incident
- Have a defined IT continuity plan for all VBFs
- Communication with all relevant stakeholders, timely and professionally
- Defined escalation plan, mentioning how escalation should happen
- Defined SMEs contacts list with email IDs and phone numbers
- Effective risk analysis procedures incorporated into major incident management process
- Post implementation review (PIR) of every major incident
- Documentation of learnings in SOPs and knowledge articles
- Education and awareness program on every major incident

Priority calculation for incidents

Priority calculation is the activity which identifies the importance of incidents based on impact and urgency, and defines a ranking system. It is calculated by the formulae as mentioned below:

Priority = Impact * Urgency; Priority = (Impact + Urgency) / 2

But today, organizations and the operational teams have a challenge in assessing and understanding the impact. Hence, here is my opinion to assess the impact of the incidents with the below mentioned factors:

- Number of users affected
- Number of external users affected
- Number of IT services affected
- Number of applications affected and number of applications managed by the service provider
- Number of departments or organizational units affected
- Did the incident occur in service/working hours?
- Is it associated with the VBF/CBU?

Each of the above factor can be prioritized/rated as 1, 2, 3, 4; 1 as the highest rating and 4 as the lowest.

Here, in the following, is a more detailed explanation on how the impact can be estimated:

Factors	Number	Ratings
Number of users affected	100	2
		(Organizations can define the rating schema; for example if the number of users affected are 500, then it can be defined with the highest rating as 1.
		If the number of users affected are 100, then it can be defined with the rating as 2.
		If the number of users affected are 50, then it can be defined with the rating as 3.
		If the number of users affected are 10 or less than 10, then it can defined

		with the lowest rating as 4.) *Based on the number of users in the organization, this can be customized.*
Number of external users affected (customers, partners, suppliers, etc.)	50	3 (Organizations can define the rating schema; for example, if the number of external users affected are 500, then you can define the highest rating as 1. If the number of external users affected are 100, then you can define the rating as 2. If the number of external users affected are 50, then you can define the rating as 3.

		If the number of external users affected are 10 or less than 10, then you can define the lowest rating as 4.) *Based on the number of external users associated with the organization, this can be customized.*
Number of IT services affected (communication service, storage service, network service, etc.)	Network service	1 (Organizations can define their rating schema; for example, if the network service is down or has any issues, this can be rated as 1. If the storage service is down or has any issues, this can be rated as 2.

		If the communication service is down or has any issues, this can be rated as 3, etc.
Number of applications affected and number of applications managed by the service provider	10 and 15	10/15 = 0.66 Rating here is based on the number of applications affected with respect to applications provided by the service provider. Here it is 10/15 which equals to 0.66 If the Value > 0.75, this can be rated as 1; If the Value > 0.5, this can be rated as 2;

		If the Value > 0.3, this can be rated as 3; If the Value > 0.1, this can be rated as 4;
Number of departments or organizational units affected	5	1 Imagining if the organization has 5 departments and 5 departments have been affected, then it can be rated as 1. Imagining if the organization has 5 departments and 3 departments have been affected, then it can be rated as 2.

| | | Imagining if the organization has 5 departments and 2 departments have been affected, then it can be rated as 3.

Imagining if the organization has 5 departments and 1 department has been affected, then the rating is 4. |
| --- | --- | --- |
| Did the incident occur in service/ working hours? | Yes / No | Yes - defines that the incident has big impact

No - defines that the incident has less impact |
| Is it associated with the VBF/ CBU | Yes/ No | Yes - defines that the incident has big impact |

		No - defines that the incident has less impact

Urgency can be identified directly by referring the SLAs with respect to the service as mentioned below:

Factors	Numbers	Ratings
What is the urgency time frame defined as per SLAs	1 hour Timeframe values can be defined as 1 hour, 4 hours, 1 day, 3 days, 7 days;	1 hour - 1; 4 hours - 2; 1 day - 3; 3 days - 4; 7 days - 5

Reports for incident management

Reports for incident management can be categorized into 4 types as:

1. Incident assortment

2. Incident CTI

3. Incident phases

4. Average incident resolution time by category

Reports on incident assortment

Reports on incident assortment should provide information on the different assortments like major incidents, P1 incidents, normal incidents, etc.

This report should capture information like:

- Total number of major incidents and its respective details like incident id, when did it occur, where did it occur, cause, etc.

- Total number of P1 incidents and its respective details like incident id, when did it occur, where did it occur, cause, etc.

- Total number of normal incidents and its respective details like incident id, when did it occur, where did it occur, cause, etc.

- Total number of security related incidents and its respective details like incident id, when did it occur, where did it occur, cause, etc.

- Total number of incidents that triggered due to inappropriate availability and its respective details like incident id, when did it occur, where did it occur, cause, etc.

- Total number of incidents that triggered due to inappropriate performance and its respective details like incident id, when did it occur, where did it occur, cause, etc.

Reports on incident category, type and item (CTI)

Reports on incident CTI should provide information on its category, type, and item structure. It should provide complete details about the category like: *hardware, software, etc.*

Types like: *servers, databases, mainframes, applications, communication devices, etc.*

Items like: router, network cable, unix, salesforce, etc.

For example:

Category	Type	Item
Hardware	Communication devices	Router

This report should capture information like:

- Total number of incidents on a specific CTI structure like 'hardware', 'communication devices' and 'router' and its respective details like incident id, when did it occur, where did it occur, assigned to, etc.

Reports on incident phases

Reports on incident phases should provide information on the incident tickets with respect to its phases.

This report should capture information like:

- Total number of incidents tickets in registered phase and its details like incident id, assigned to, etc.

- Total number of incidents tickets in diagnosis phase and its details like incident id, assigned to, etc.

- Total number of incidents tickets in resolution phase and its details like incident id, assigned to, etc.

- Total number of incidents tickets in waiting for customer's approval phase and its details like incident id, assigned to, etc.

- Total number of incidents tickets in closed phase and its details like incident id, assigned to, etc.

Reports on incident resolution time

Reports on incident resolution time should provide information about the incident id, priority of the incident, time taken to resolve the incident, associated SLA, SLA adherence, and the details of the incident analysts who resolved the issue.

Process flow for incident management

Process flow for incident management defines a sequence of activities that will result in effective incident management operations aiming at quicker resolution of issues or outages.

Generally in an IT organization, incidents can be detected and raised by end user/ customer, service desk staff, incident management team, 3rd party vendor who is a stakeholder of the IT project, and operations team.

End user: Is the user who is actually using the IT services.

Customer: Is the person or a team who is paying the money for the receiving IT services.

Service Desk Staff: Single point of contact for addressing the issues of users and customers.

L2/ L3 team: Point of contact for resolving the issues as per the defined SLA's.

3rd party vendor: Another company who is associated with an IT service provider, to deliver IT services to the customer.

Operations team: A team of the IT service provider, who are involved in monitoring kind of activities.

Process Flow - Incident Resolution by L1

Activity 1:

Service Desk / Incident management detects the incident from the user or customer through phone call/ email/ chat interaction.

Activity 2:

Service desk/ Incident management team verifies if the caller or requester is an authorized user and categorizes whether if the issue is an incident/ service request.

Activity 3:

If its determined as an incident, then more details regarding the incident is gathered.

Activity 4:

Service desk/ Incident management team checks whether if its new incident or already logged incident.

Activity 5:

Accordingly an incident ticket is raised in the service management tool, with complete description, impact, urgency, etc.

Activity 6:

Service desk/ Incident management team checks its knowledge base and tries to resolve the issue if it's in their scope. If its not in their scope, then the ticket is assigned to L2/L3 team.

Activity 7:

After troubleshooting, if the issue is resolved then the ticket is resolved.

Activity 8:

After setting the incident ticket in resolved status, after 3 days of time then the ticket is closed.

Note: If the user/ customer has any issue with the resolved ticket, then the ticket is reopened.

Process Flow - Incident Resolution by L2/ L3

Service desk/ Incident management team checks its knowledge base and tries to resolve the issue if it's not in their scope, then the ticket is assigned to L2/L3 team.

Activity 1:

L2 team verifies if the troubleshooting is done on the correct CI.

Activity 2:

L2 team checks if it's a critical or major incident. If it's a major incident, it is assigned to major incident team.

Activity 3:

L2 team gathers complete information about the CI using the CMDB and historical incidents.

Activity 4:

If L2/L3 team is not able to resolve the issue, then they contact the vendor.

Activity 5:

A 3rd part company or vendor is involved and their help is taken to resolve the issue.

Activity 6:

Once the issue is resolved, the troubleshooting steps performed by the 3rd party company are documented and sent as knowledge articles for the knowledge manager to publish it as a knowledge article.

Activity 7:

After setting the incident ticket in resolved status, after 3 days of time then the ticket is closed.

Activity 8:

After setting the incident ticket in resolved status, after 3 days of time then the ticket is closed.

Note: If the user/ customer has any issue with the resolved ticket, then the ticket is reopened.

Process flow for major incident management

Process flow for major incident management defines a sequence of activities that will result in effective major incident management operations aiming at quicker resolution of issues or outages.

Generally in an IT organization, major incidents are created by incident management team after carefully understanding the issue.

Process Flow – Major Incident Resolution

Activity 1:

Major incident management team receives an alert about major incident.

Activity 2:

Major incident management team consolidates all information about the incident and determines whether if it's a major incident.

Activity 3:

If it's determined that it's a major incident, Major incident management team communicates it to the customer management and the relevant stakeholders through email.

Activity 4:

Major incident management team opens the bridge call, inviting all the relevant technical SME's also 3rd party company of the CI (if necessary).

Activity 5:

Once the issue is resolved, the bridge call is closed and informed to all the stakeholders and customer management that the issue has been resolved.

Activity 6:

Accordingly a problem ticket is also raised to understand the RCA and to identify the permanent fix.

Activity 7:

Once the end user is satisfied, document all the troubleshooting steps and send it to knowledge manager for publishing a knowledge article.

Activity 8:

A review meeting is conducted on the major incident like a PIR, to understand what went good and bad. Accordingly lessons learnt are shared with the stakeholders.

Incident Management for Consultants and Management

Implementation of incident management process

Define

Prepare the project charter, consisting of a business case, SOW, MOSCOW analysis, goal statement, project plan, project scope, and roles and responsibilities.

Opportunity Statement – should define the issues in existing IT management/operations like:

* SLA breaches

* Lack of knowledge materials or reference materials or no knowledge base

* No standard process and procedures defined

* Customer dissatisfaction ratings

* Escalations and penalizations

Business case – should describe the benefits and opportunities of incident management considering the following areas:

* What are the customer expectations like Csat, MTRS, etc.?

* What are the short term benefits and long term benefits of this project?

* Does this new initiative align with other business processes, if any exist?

103

- What impacts will this new initiative have on other business units and employees? Pros and cons.

- Should we have an explicit incident management function or integrated service desk and incident management?

- What are the risks and issues involved and what are the dependencies?

- Estimations of costs on infrastructure assets (hardware, software, people-ware) and other miscellaneous things.

MOSCOW analysis - Should capture the requirements with respect to Must, Should, Could, and Would be (in future).

Statement of work (SOW) - Develop the SOW for the incident management process, defining the:

- Scope of services/products for which incident management applies.

- Identification of service assets and CIs that are out of scope.

- Hardware, software and people required to manage IM as a process and operations.

Goal statement – should be closely associated with the prepared business case and SOW. Goals should be SMART and mention:

- What are the CSFs?

- What are the KPIs?

- What is the time estimated to see the results?

Project interfaces - should define the boundaries, scope, and relationships of the Incident management with other ITSM processes and functions.

Project plan - should show the timeline and milestones for various activities to establish incident management process and run the operations.

Roles and responsibilities - should identify the required roles and hire the human resources. Primary roles needed for Incident management, can be defined as:

- Level 1 incident analysts.

- Level 2 incident analysts.

- Incident manager.

- Major incident manager.

- Incident management process owner.

Also define RACI model for clarity in roles and responsibilities.

Measure

Measure phase should define the metrics and measurement plan, for capturing the performance of IM process and operations. These metrics should be defined based on the customer requirements and acceptance criteria.

- Define measurement plan that addresses:

    - Who will do the measurement? (Incident manager, Incident analysts, etc.)
    - What services will be measured?
    - How will it be measured?
    - How often will it be measured? (Daily, Weekly, Monthly)
    - How will it be reported (PowerPoint presentation, Charts, Reports, etc.)

- Define metrics for incident management with respect to:

    - Critical to quality (Customer satisfaction, MTRS, MTBSI, etc.)
    - Critical to process (Process adherence, defects in process, etc.)
    - Critical to cost (Number of resources involved, Cost associated with an incident, etc.)
    - Critical to delivery (Number of incidents, number of major incidents)
    To know more details on metrics, check the section Metrics.

- Ensure those metrics are SMART (Specific, Measurable, Achievable, Relevant and Time-bound).

- Define SLAs for incident management consulting SLM, and other ITSM processes (like Availability management, Capacity management, Information security management, Supplier management, etc.) as per customer's requirements. Best practice on definition of SLAs:

  - ❖ For Greenfield project, define SLAs after understanding the operations for at least 2 months.
  - ❖ If there are any experienced staff who worked as an Incident manager, you can take his experiences and baseline the SLAs - ensuring you could redefine them (if necessary) after checking 2 months of operations.
  - ❖ You can have a brainstorming session with all ITSM process owners and define SLAs - ensuring you could redefine them (if necessary) after checking 2 months of operations.

Analyze

Analyze phase should define high level process designs (linking customer requirements and acceptance criteria) identifying inputs, outputs, outcomes, triggers, interfaces, boundaries, exceptions, roles, etc.

- Understand the existing IT services to categorize and organize them to a hierarchy.

- Define the high level IM process with inputs, outputs, outcomes, triggers, interfaces, roles and responsibilities, etc.

- Define the high level process for major incident management with inputs, outputs, outcomes, triggers, interfaces, roles and responsibilities, etc.

Design

Design phase should define the detailed and complete process and procedures

- Define a detailed hierarchy for organizing the incidents

E.g.:

Hardware
desktop and accessories
laptop and accessories
servers and accessories
networking devices

Software
Operating system
Applications
Middleware
Databases

- Define procedures for handling minor, normal, and major incidents with respect to different IT services.

- Define the IM process phases with respect to the best practices like ITIL, MOF, etc.

For example:

- ❖ Registration and categorization → Determine if this is a new incident (check the KEDB) → Correlate to the previously logged incident → Resolution (Apply the resolution procedures defined in KEDB) → Confirmation from the customer → Closure
- ❖ Registration and categorization → Determine if this is a new incident (figured out not a new incident) → Assignment → Diagnosis (figured out that it would need technical expertise) → Functional/hierarchical escalation → Resolution → Confirmation from the customer → Closure
- ❖ Registration and categorization → Determine if this is a new incident (figured out not a new incident) → Assignment → Diagnosis (troubleshooting performed) → Resolution → Confirmation from the customer → Closure
- ❖ Registration and categorization → Determine if this is a new incident (figured out not a new incident) → Assignment → Diagnosis → Assignment to third party company → Verify the resolution performed by third party → Confirmation from the customer → Closure

- Develop incident models for different IT services, defining:

  - ❖ Steps to resolve an incident
  - ❖ Responsibilities of IM team

- Develop email notification templates to inform PM staff, giving complete details on the incident.

- Define procedures for effective incident diagnosis on different services.

109

- Define a policy on who should create incident record and when should the incident record be created.

- Define the rules for reopening any incidents.

- Define a knowledge base with all technical knowledge with respect to different services.

- Define the conditions for normal, minor and major incidents.

- Define communication procedures for handling major incidents.

- Select the group of L2 analysts, who will be part of MIM.

- Define the impact and urgency levels as per the business requirements.

  For example:

Impact	Affected users
1	More than 100 users
2	More than 50 users
3	More than 10 users
4	1-2 users

Urgency	To be resolved in
1	Less than 30 minutes
2	Less than 1 hour
3	Less than 3 hours
4	Less than 2 days

- Define a separate repository for incidents, IMIS (incident management information system), to store incident records.

- Define appropriate ITSM or incident management tool with respect to business requirements.

- Define what all details have to be encapsulated in incident records.

  - ❖ details from service desk (caller name, caller location, primary contact name, calling on behalf of, date and time of the call)
  - ❖ incident registration number
  - ❖ description of the incident
  - ❖ detailed description
  - ❖ affected services
  - ❖ affected configuration items or service
  - ❖ impact
  - ❖ urgency
  - ❖ diagnosis performed
  - ❖ time and date of troubleshooting
  - ❖ date and time of closure
  - ❖ customer's confirmation to close the incident
  - ❖ lessons learnt

- Define email and announcements templates for IT critical outage notifications.

- Define IT contacts list responsible for different services (e.g. network, application server, etc.).

- Define trainings on process, tools, technical knowledge, etc.

- Execute the incident management operations.

Validate

Validate phase should define the V&V (verification and validation) and improvement activities to improve the IM process.

- Ensure all the process collaterals are approved by the Service manager and other ITSM process owners.

- Take feedback from all ITSM stakeholders on the definition new processes and procedures.

- Prioritize and act on the feedbacks and recommendations, if they make sense.

- Define procedures for IM staff and other ITSM stakeholders to give recommendations and feedback on the defined system.

- Ensure all incidents are registered, categorized, tracked, and closed in the ITSM tool as per defined procedures.

- Ensure the IT contacts list is regularly updated with all the necessary contact details.

- Ensure the incident management operation is in consideration with metrics and SLT's defined in SLAs.

- Verify that all unresolved issues are tracked and escalated to the next level of supervision in consideration with SLAs.

Improving incident management process

Define

Define phase should define the improvement opportunities, business case, goal statement, project plan, and roles and responsibilities.

Customer expectations – Understand the customer expectations like Csat, MTRS, MTTR, etc.

Opportunity Statement – should define the issues in existing incident management operations like:

- SLA breaches

- Lack of knowledge materials or no knowledge base

- No process definition or inefficient process definition

- Customer dissatisfaction

- Escalations

Business case - should describe the benefits and opportunities of improving incident management considering the following areas:

- What are the short term benefits and long term benefits of this project?

- What impacts will this new initiative have on other business units and employees? Pros and cons.

- Should we have an explicit incident management or integrated incident management and problem management?

- Reason for initiating this improvement project should include:

  - ❖ Number of incidents being reported every month in service desk.
  - ❖ Number of unresolved issues in service desk.
  - ❖ Number of incidents that resulted in penalization.
  - ❖ Number of incidents that resulted in SLA breaches.
  - ❖ Number of incidents that defamed the organization.
  - ❖ Estimations of costs on the improvement initiative.

Goal statement – should be focused on business goals and IT goals

- Should define what is the improvement team aiming to accomplish?

- What is the estimated time for delivery of results?

- What are the tangible results deliverables?

Project plan - should show the milestones and time estimation for the activities involved in improving incident management as a process and operations.

Roles and responsibilities - should identify the required roles. Primary roles needed for Incident management, can be defined as:

- Incident manager.

- Major incident manager.

- Level 1 incident analysts.

- Level 2 incident analysts.

Define RACI model for clarity in roles and responsibilities.

Measure

Measure phase should capture as much as information about the current operations to understand how and how well it is being operated. It also includes setting up the baselines as the basis for improvement.

- Identify the frequency of incidents.

- Identify number of normal incidents, major incidents, and minor incidents.

- Identify which services are creating maximum number of incidents.

- Understand the IT services running in the organization.

- Understand the scope of services for incident management.

- Determine if the current scope is good enough for IM.

- Understand how the BIA is estimated.

- Understand the existing IM process.

115

- Understand the major incidents and areas/services where it occurred.

- Identify the P1 and P2 incidents and categorize them into groups (incidents with respect to databases, incidents with respect to networks, incidents related to power outages, incidents related to application servers, etc.).

- Analyze the previous incidents which received positive CSAT.

- Check with the IM staff on whether if they have clarity and understanding on the processes and procedures.

- Talk with IM staff personnel's who received positive CSATs to check what was good/bad and what was missing in the existing IM process.

- Analyze the previous incidents that breached the SLAs.

- Analyze the previous incidents that had received negative CSAT.

- Talk with IM staff personnel's who received negative CSATs to check what was good/bad and what was missing in the existing IM process (where he made his own individual decision in dealing the incident).

- Analyze the existing metrics and SLAs, if they are feasible.

- Perform baselines of the current IM operations.

Analyze

Analyze phase should identify the gaps and root causes for the discrepancies in IM process and operations. It also includes analyzing if the process collaterals were well defined like processes, RACI matrix, SOPs, CSFs, KPIs, metrics, etc.

- Analyze which services are creating maximum number of incidents.

- Identify the cause of the incidents and why they breached SLAs.

- Identify the root causes why the incidents breached the SLAs.

    ❖ Determine if there was enough reference materials available in the knowledge base and if the knowledge in reference materials was technically accurate.
    ❖ Were there any contact details discrepancies?
    ❖ Was the IM staff unaware of the process and procedures?

- Identify the flaws or misses in the existing process with respect to the business scenario checking:

    ❖ If the process is aligned to business objectives.
    ❖ If the process provides clarity in roles and responsibilities.
    ❖ If the process is complete, and there is enough guidance for all the scenarios that can happen in the incident lifecycle.
    For example:
      ➢ Registration and categorization → Determine if this is a new incident (check the KEDB) → Correlate to

117

the previously logged incident → Resolution (Apply the resolution procedures defined in KEDB) → Confirmation from the customer → Closure

➢ Registration and categorization → Determine if this is a new incident (figured out not a new incident) → Assignment → Diagnosis (figured out that it would need technical expertise) → Functional/hierarchical escalation → Resolution → Confirmation from the customer → Closure

➢ Registration and categorization → Determine if this is a new incident (figured out not a new incident) → Assignment → Diagnosis (troubleshooting performed) → Resolution → Confirmation from the customer → Closure

➢ Registration and categorization → Determine if this is a new incident (figured out not a new incident) → Assignment → Diagnosis → Assignment to third party company → Verify the resolution performed by third party → Confirmation from the customer → Closure

❖ The process is clearly written without any ambiguity
❖ The process is aligned to the best practices and standards
❖ The process is repeatable

Note: Analysis on all the above activities can be done by brainstorming with the key stakeholders of change management team, ITSMO (IT Service management officer), ITSM manager and IT manager.

Improve

Improve phase aims at improving the current IM process and operations with creative solutions to eliminate the root causes in order to fix and prevent process and operational discrepancies.

- Involve all the key stakeholder from IM and other ITSM process and brainstorm how to improve the IM process and operations.

- List all the discussed ideas and propose your ideas:

  - ❖ Redefine the CSFs, KPIs and metrics consulting SLM as per the customer's requirements. Metrics should be defined in alignment to:
    - ➤ Customer's priorities, requirements, and acceptance criteria

    - ➤ Most important services

  - ❖ Redefine the IM process ensuring:
    - ➤ There is a clear definition and demarcation on what is an incident, what is service request, and what is standard change.

    - ➤ There is clear definition and conditions for normal and major incidents.

    - ➤ There is clear definition on impact, urgency, and prioritization.

    - ➤ There is clear definition of inputs, triggers, outputs, and interfaces for the process.

    - ➤ There is clear definition of incident models for different services.

> ➢ There is IT contacts list responsible for different services (e.g. network, application server, etc.).

> ➢ There is appropriate estimation method for BIA.

> ➢ There is a defined procedure for creating incident record in IMIS (incident management information system).

> ➢ There are workflows/flowcharts that are easily understandable.

- Seek approvals from the Service Manager & Process owner on the redefined process collaterals.

- Ensure every IM staff is aware on the usage of the service management tool.

- Define policies to conduct training on process, technical knowledge, tool knowledge, etc.

- Define policies to assess staff knowledge, conducting exams, quizzes, etc.

- Implement event management tools to identify the incidents as soon as they incept.

- Define automation techniques in event management tools for resolving the discrepancies on CIs and Services.

Control

Control phase defines the V&V (verification and validation) and continuous improvement activities that should be performed on IM processes and operations.

- Monitor the IM operations for the next 2 months - ensuring all the IM staff follows the defined processes and procedures.

- Check if the number of operations staff involved in IM is good to manage the number of incidents occurring.

- Ensure that the IM staff is aware of the SLAs for all services.

- Check if the IM staff is able to meet the defined metrics and SLAs.

- Ensure all incidents are being tracked in the SM tool.

- Check for the incidents which have breached the SLAs and perform the root cause analysis.

- Document the lessons learned.

- Update the process again if there were any changes in the business requirements.

- Prepare monthly reports (including accomplishments, targets met as per SLA, targets breached, major incidents logged and resolved, major incidents that are unresolved and WIP (Work In Progress); it should include financial information about the incidents and incidents that are unresolved).

- Check if the redefined IM process meets the expectations in terms of SLAs and CSAT.

121

- Collect feedback from IM staff and customers.

Integrating incident management with other ITSM processes and functions

ITSM processes can of course be integrated with other ITSM processes and functions which will enable in reducing the costs on human resources.

Here is a list of scenarios where IM can be integrated with other processes and functions:

IM and SD

Integration of IM and SD is very much possible, provided there is demarcation of roles and responsibilities and SOPs for the staff in the integrated process. This can be done by assigning:

L1 and L2 analysts to manage the service desk calls ensuring they act as a point of contact for customer concerns and trying to restore the services quickly while aiming at customer satisfaction. They will refer the KEDB's and KB to provide solutions for issues of the customers.

Incident analysts will handle those escalated calls on technical issues where there is no reference materials available in KEDB and KB. Incident analysts will check the EM tools, capacity management tools, availability management tools, and will try to resolve the incidents using their technical expertise.

And major incident manager will handle those major incidents as agreed in the SLAs.

An incident manager will be accountable person for all the operations of L1 and L2 analysts, Incident analysts, and the Major Incident Manager.

IM and PM

Integration of IM and PM is very much possible, provided there is demarcation of roles and responsibilities in integrated process. This can be done by assigning responsibilities as mentioned below:

L1 analysts will handle the incidents in an attempt to restore services quickly as soon as possible. They will check the EM tools (to understand when the incident occurred, which CI has caused the discrepancy, what events did it generate), capacity management tools and availability management tools (to understand the capacity and availability configuration), and will try to resolve the incidents with their technical expertise.

L2 analysts will handle those unresolved/unknown underlying root causes of incidents. If L1 analysts cannot resolve any issue, and if they feel that it's out of their scope, those incidents will be assigned to L2 analysts.

Before assigning any incident to L2 analysts, L1 analysts should provide all the troubleshooting steps performed and investigation done, so that L2 analysts don't repeat those steps. Now, L2 analysts will work with other processes stakeholders and SME's to identify temporary fixes and permanent fixes while identifying the root cause of the issue. L2 analysts should be the most technical and experienced folks with respect to L1 analysts.

A major incident manager will handle those issues which have great impact and cause big financial losses.

Operations manager will be accountable for all the operations of L1 analysts and L2 analysts.

IM and EM

Integration of IM and EM is very much possible, provided there is demarcation of roles and responsibilities and SOPs for the staff in integrated process. This can be done by assigning:

L1 analysts to monitor the events on event management tools and inform (through phone calls/email/etc.) the respective ITSM stakeholders.

L2 analysts will handle incidents checking the EM tools, capacity management tools, availability management tools, and will try to resolve the incidents using their technical expertise.

A major incident manager will handle those issues which have major impact.

An incident manager will be the accountable person for all the operations of L1 analysts, L2 analysts.

Sizing incident management operations team

Right sized incident management team means a team which has the right number of human resources to carry out IM operations effectively and efficiently while meeting business objectives without breaching any SLAs.

This right size for an incident management team can be estimated based on few factors like:

- Number of services offered and its associated end users
- Total number of end users who would be using the services
- Historical data with respect to the number of IM resources
- Historical data with respect to the number of incidents
- Associated SLAs

But the best way to define the number of IM analysts would be based on the number of incidents in a month, as per historical data and its associated SLAs.

For example: If my historical data says that there are 100 major incidents in a month and 1200 normal incidents.

Assuming SLA for major incidents is 30 minutes.

Assuming SLA for P1 incidents is 1 hour; P2 incidents is 1 day; P3 incidents is 2 days; P4 incidents is 3 days;

100 major incidents in a month can be derived as 3.3 incidents per day, assuming it as 3 incidents per day. Now assuming the worst case scenario, where 3 incidents occurred at the same time; I would define a separate team for major incident management which consists of 3 members which includes 1 as major incident manager, and other 2 as major incident analysts/ coordinators.

Out of 1200 normal incidents, let's assume there are 250 - P1 incidents, 500 - P2 incidents, 250 - P3 incidents, and 200 - P4 incidents.

Now 250 P1 incidents in a month can be derived as 8.6 or 9 incidents / day, and the SLA is 1 hour; as it is P1 incidents, I wouldn't take any chances. Even assuming the worst case scenario, where 9 incidents occurred at the same time; I would define 9 members for handling the P1 incidents.

Now 500 P2 incidents in a month can be derived as 16.6 or 17 incidents / day, and the SLA is 1 day; as it is P2 incidents, I have good time. Here I would assign only 1 member. (If there are no P1 incidents at an instance or if any members out of 9 are free they would look into P2 incidents)

Now 250 P3 incidents in a month can be derived as 8.3 or 8 incidents / day, and the SLA is 2 days; as it is P3 incidents, I have enough time. Here I would assign only 1 member. (If there are no P1 incidents at an instance or if any members out of 9 are free they would look into P3 incidents as well)

Now 200 P4 incidents in a month can be derived as 6.6 or 7 incidents / day, and the SLA is 4 days; as it is P4 incidents, I have plenty of time. Here I would assign only 1 member. (If there are no P1 incidents at an instance or if any members out of 9 are free they would look into P4 incidents as well)

So totally the ideal team size for managing 1200 incidents and 100 major incidents would be 15 which includes 1 incident manager and 1 major incident manager. (Also considering the attendance issues or issues like sick leave/casual leave, etc.)

Note: This doesn't mean, I am proposing a specific team for P1, P2, P3, P4 incidents, that was just for my calculations; so there is only one incident management team taking care of all P1, P2, P3, P4 incidents.

Fishbone diagram for incident management

Fishbone diagram or Cause and effect analysis diagram is a problem analysis tool that can be used to analyze the issues in any IT operations. This diagram represents to a fish bone, depicting the causes and effects for a specific problem statement. This method breaks down the problem into sequential layers of detail that potentially contribute to a particular effect. It also helps us to work on each cause prior to finding the root cause.

This diagram can be constructed through a simple approach by defining the problem, brainstorming, and identifying the causes.

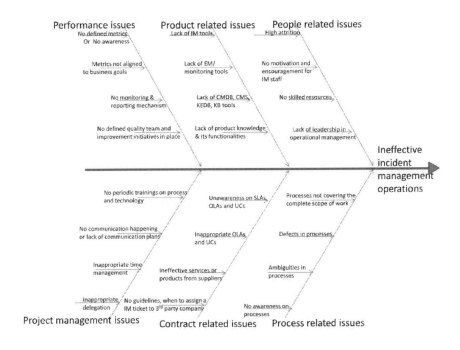

Fishbone diagram for ineffective incident management operations can be represented by the below mentioned causes:

- **People related issues**

    People related issues can be segregated into issues like *high attrition, no motivation and encouragement for IM staff, no skilled and knowledgeable resources, lack of leadership, etc.*

- **Process related issues**

    Process related issues can be segregated into issues like *ineffective processes (which doesn't cover the complete scope of work), defects in processes, ambiguities in processes, no awareness on processes, etc.*

- **Product related issues**

    Product related issues can be segregated issues like *lack of IM tools, lack of event management or monitoring tools, lack of CMDB, CMS, KEDB, and KB tools, Lack of product/tool knowledge and its functionalities, etc.*

- **Contract related issues**

    Contract related issues can be classified into issues like *Unawareness on SLAs, OLAs and UCs, Inappropriate OLAs and UCs, Ineffective services or products delivered from suppliers, no defined guidelines when to assign a IM ticket to a 3rd party company, etc.*

- **Performance issues**

    Performance related issues can be classified into issues like *no defined metrics or no awareness, metrics not aligned to business goals, no monitoring and reporting mechanism, no defined quality team and improvement initiatives in place, etc.*

- **Project management issues**

  Project management issues can be classified into issues like *no periodic trainings on process and technology, no communication plan in place or no communication happening to stakeholders, inappropriate time management, inappropriate delegation, etc.*

Incident management in clouds

Incident management process for clouds

Incident in cloud

Any breakdown or outage in cloud services is called an incident. It also includes reduction in the quality of cloud services. Incidents in clouds can be caused by failure of hardware, software, networking devices and connections. These incidents can be classified into 2 types as: Infrastructure incidents and ND (natural disaster) incidents.

Infrastructure incidents: Incidents that are caused by inadequate infrastructure design and planning because of hardware, software, virus, malware, and hackers can be treated as infrastructure incidents.

ND (Natural Disaster) incidents: Incidents that are caused by natural disasters like storms, tsunamis, earth quakes, etc. can be treated as ND (natural disaster) incidents.

Incident management process for cloud

Incident management for clouds is a standard process for registering, categorizing, analyzing, diagnosing, resolving and closing the incidents in cloud environment. The prime responsibility of incident management for clouds is to resolve the failures of CIs or cloud components and restore the cloud services as soon as possible.

Incident management process for clouds is the sequence of activities which results in quick resolution (to restore normal functionality) and closure of the incident in cloud environment. It involves the below mentioned activities:

Reporting → Registration and categorization → Diagnosis → Escalation → Resolution → Closure

Reporting and Registration

This activity defines the procedure on how the incident initiator or any IT stakeholder has reported an incident (incidents can be reported by a phone call/email/fax/ITSM tool). It is the initial phase which defines how the incident has been informed, who has informed, what is the incident, when did it happen, where did it happen, etc. It ensures that all reported incidents are logged in a tool, categorized, assigned, and tracked in order to follow up for future references. Primary questions that should be asked from the incident initiator are:

- Who is reporting the issue?

- What is the issue/failure about? With which application/software/database/etc. is the error message associated?

- What is the cloud model used by the user? Where has the failure or issue occurred (private/public/hybrid/community cloud)?

- What is the cloud service with which the user is enrolled? In which service did the failure occur (SaaS, IaaS, HaaS, etc.)?

- What device is the user using (Computer, Smartphone, or Gadget)?

- What is the browser? Can the user retry using another browser?

- How did the user encounter the issue? Did the initiator install/uninstall any new hardware or software?

- Is there any error message; if yes, what is the error message that he/she is seeing?

- Can the user send the error message he/she is seeing?

- Is it just happening with him/her or any other users (he/she is aware of)?

- How long has it been happening?

Mandatory fields for reporting and registration phase that would be helpful for Cloud Service Management tools are:

- Incident initiator name

- Location of the Incident initiator

- Primary contact name

- Calling on behalf of

- Contact number

- Date and time

- Brief description of the incident

- Detailed description

- Affected services as per user's view

- Affected configuration items or services as per user's view

- Affected location

- Impact as per user's view

- Urgency as per user's view

- Cloud service (SaaS, PaaS, IaaS)

- Cloud model (Private, Public, Hybrid)

- Incident registration number

- Assigned to (every incident is assigned to a specific team member so that every incident gets the attention of an individual to resolve the incident quickly)

- Assigned department (you can also assign an incident to a group when you are not sure about the available team member)

Analysis and categorization

This activity analyzes the incident information to understand the details of what is the incident in reality, what are impacted services in reality, whether if there was any such incident before, whether if there is any known error and workaround/solution for this kind of incident.

Analysis of the incident can be performed by understanding:

- What is the issue, outage, or failure (with complete details and description)?

- Where did the issue happen (private cloud, public cloud, community cloud, or hybrid cloud)?

- In which service (SaaS, IaaS, PaaS, etc.) did the issue happen?

138

- In which cloud model did the issue happen?

- Is there any connection between other incidents?

And by performing

- 5 why analysis

- By checking the event management/monitoring tools

- Chronological analysis

- BIA (Business Impact Analysis) checking the CMDB

- Check in CMS and CMDB to understand if there were any previous incidents, changes, etc.

Categorization classifies the incidents for providing meticulous analysis and investigation by SME's which helps in resolving the incidents quickly. Incidents can be categorized based on:

- cloud services

- cloud deployment models

- CI/Service which triggered the incident

Mandatory fields for analysis and categorization phase that would be helpful for Cloud Service Management tools are:

- Incident initiator name

- Location of the Incident initiator

- Primary contact name

- Contact number

- Registered Incident number

- Detailed description

- Affected services in reality

- Affected configuration items in reality

- Incident occurred in which cloud service (SaaS, PaaS, IaaS, etc.)

- Incident occurred in which model (Public, Private, Hybrid, etc.)

- Location of failed CI

- Impact (Number of users affected)

- Urgency as per SLAs

- Details of analysis (Performed by the incident analyst)

- BIA priority (1,2,3,4)

- Is it a major incident?

- Is that a third party supplier's issue?

- Event management/monitoring tool's references (Event numbers, CI which generated the event, Reason for the event, etc.)

- Categorization of incidents (based on the analysis like hardware/software issue, etc.)

- Assigned to (every incident is assigned to a specific team member so that every incident gets the attention of an individual to resolve the incident quickly)

- Assigned department (you can also assign an incident to a group when you are not sure about the available team member)

Diagnosis and Escalation

This activity performs deep dive analysis on the incident, triggered CI and error message/logs that are generated by the service or configuration item.

Diagnosis can be performed by:

- Contacting the respective SME's (If the incident is related to capacity, contact the Capacity staff. If the incident is related to availability, contact the availability staff. If the incident is related to networks, contact the network admin/ SME)

- Contacting the cloud architect/developers who developed the respective service

Escalation determines whether if the incident has to be escalated functionally or hierarchically.

In hierarchical escalation, an incident analyst determines that he/she cannot fix the issue as its beyond his/her technical expertise or some extra access privileges are required; then, the incident will be hierarchically escalated to higher authorities in his/her team.

In functional escalation, an incident analyst determines that the issue cannot be fixed by his/her team and as a result it will be functionally escalated to another department.

Mandatory fields for diagnosis and escalation phase that would be helpful for Cloud Service Management tools are:

- Registered Incident number

- Detailed description

- Incident occurred in which cloud service (SaaS, PaaS, IaaS, etc.)

- Incident occurred in which model (Public, Private, Hybrid, etc.)

- Location of failed CI

- Impact (Number of users affected)

- Urgency as per SLAs

- Details of analysis (Performed by the incident analyst)

- BIA priority (1,2,3,4)

- Is it a major incident?

- Is that a third party supplier's issue?

- Event management/ monitoring tool's references (Event numbers, CI which generated the event, Reason for the event, etc.)

- Categorization of incidents (based on the analysis like hardware/software issue, etc.)

- Error message and screenshots of the failed CI

- Initial analysis performed by

- Initial analysis performed by which team

- Details of analysis (Performed by the incident analyst)

- Escalation type

- Reason for escalation

- Escalated to

- Escalated department (you can also assign an incident to a group, when you are not sure about the available team member)

- Does it require any third party SME?

- Details of diagnosis performed

Resolution

This activity resolves the technical or generic failures caused by a configuration item or IT service and restores normal functionality.

Incident analysts log all the troubleshooting steps that were performed to resolve the incident.

Mandatory fields for resolution phase that would be helpful for Cloud Service Management tools are:

- Registered Incident number

- Detailed description

- Incident occurred in which cloud service (SaaS, PaaS, IaaS, etc.)

- Incident occurred in which model (Public, Private, Hybrid, etc.)

- Location of failed CI

- Impact (Number of users affected)

- Urgency as per SLAs

- Details of analysis (Performed by the incident analyst)

- BIA priority (1,2,3,4)

- Documentation of troubleshooting steps

- Reference material used

- Time and date of troubleshooting

- Resolved by

Closure

It is the final step in the incident management process and which closes the incident ticket created by the incident initiator.

After applying the incident resolution, incident analysts check the effectiveness of the resolution in test environments. Then, the incident is closed, and an incident record is prepared and saved in the IMIS.

Mandatory details captured in this activity are:

- Incident registration number

- Date and time of closure

- Incident manager's approval to close the incident

- Time taken to close the incident

- Did the incident breach SLA

- Was it resolved by third party?

- Cause of the incident

- Lessons learned; what went correct and what went wrong or delayed the resolution

Incident analysis in cloud

Incident analysis activity can be classified into 2 parts as information gathering and analysis as mentioned below:

Information gathering on cloud incidents

- What is the login id of the user?

- What is the issue/failure?

- Where is the user located at? In which country?

- What is the name of the application/software?

- What is the cloud service (Iaas, PaaS, SaaS, etc.) where the incident occurred? What is the cloud model where the incident occurred (private, public, etc.)?

- When was the last time he/she used this service?

- What is the URL of the application/software?

- What is the port number this application associated with?

- What was the version of the application you were using?

- What is the IP address of the application/software?

- What is the error message? How did it happen?

- What is the operating system used by the user?

- What computer/smart phone/gadget are you using? What is the manufacturer name?

- Did you install any new software or hardware? Can you uninstall the newly installed h/w or s/w and retry accessing the application/service?

Analysis on incidents

Incidents in cloud can generally occur when there are any discrepancies in applications, data, runtime, middleware, operating system, virtualization, servers, storage, and networking environments.

Initially this analysis should be conducted by performing impact analysis and diagnosis.

Impact analysis of the cloud incidents can be estimated by understanding:

- How this service is connected to other services?

- How this service is being used by other stakeholders?

- How this service supports stakeholders and other business processes?

- Are there any services depending on this service?

- What type of data would this application have (highly sensitive, confidential, or public)?

- What is the number of users using this application?

- What are the associated SLAs with respect to the service?

Diagnosis can be performed to discover the root cause of the issue, by understanding:

- Is the service accessible and available in other locations? Or is the service outage is at only one/few specific locations?

146

- Checking the event management tools or checking the active monitoring/passive monitoring tools in infrastructure,

- Checking the trace reports, error log, and event log generated by servers machines

- Checking the trace reports, error log, and event log generated by databases

- Check if there was any recent software/hardware installation on the servers

- Check if there is any issue with data packets, encryption, etc.

- Check if there is any issue with the networks and networking devices

- Check if there are any issues with cables, etc.

147

Preventing incidents in cloud

Incidents happen, and they happen due to some or the other reasons like hardware failure, software bugs, human errors, natural disasters, etc. Here are some best practices that can prevent incidents in cloud, as mentioned below:

- Defining robust capacity plans for all services and upgrading them regularly as per the demand

- Defining effective service continuity strategy and plans and regular testing

- Thorough testing before implementing any changes in the environment

- Conducting regular health assessments on all hosted services (running processes, syscalls, authentication), virtual machines (CPU load, memory usage, hypercalls, scaling behavior), and physical machines

- Network monitoring on all connections, active connections per source/destination, duration of the connections, source and destination address port, etc.

- Must ensure that authentication and authorization rules and technology is effective at protecting the information systems, tenant's resources, etc.

- Monitor the provisioning and de-provisioning of resources

- Should ensure that host operating systems and software have security patches and updates applied in a timely manner

- Security updates should also happen on BIOS, switch firmware, virtualization environments, etc.

- Guest operating systems should have security patches and updates applied in a timely manner

- Regular anti-malware scanning on guest operating systems and host systems

- Effective data encryption methodologies on all storage systems

- Monitoring the firewalls, through host based firewalls on host systems, and explicit firewall for guest operating systems

- Usage of GIS (Geographic Information Systems) technology to help the cloud service providers in identifying the potential natural disasters, and developing the corrective and preventive actions.

Advice on Incident Management Operations

Common incidents in database servers

User Unable to connect to DB Server

User connectivity issues can be resolved by:

1. Checking whether the ping request is working or not

2. Checking the credentials

   - Checking user name and password

3. Checking if the protocols are enabled or not

4. Checking if the login was created for that particular user or not

5. Checking the client and the server run on the same network protocol or not

6. Checking if the login id is disabled/expired

7. Checking if the authentication mode

8. Checking what is the maximum number of connections in connection pool

9. Check if browser service is running

Job failure incidents

Job failure incidents can be resolved by:

1. Checking if the agent service is down

2. Checking if the job's schedule is enabled

3. Checking if the Event log Services are running or not

4. Checking if the backup path is accessible or not

5. Checking if there is any process or query running on the task in parallel

6. Checking if there is any Owner change

7. Checking if there is any Permission issues

8. Checking if the Server is down

9. Checking the Disk Space

10. Checking the description from view job history

11. Check Event Viewer, Error Logs for failure causes

Backup failure incidents

Backup failure incidents can be resolved by:

1. Checking the Disk space

2. Checking if the server agent is down

3. Checking if the specified path is available for backup or not?

4. Checking if the Backup operator role is given to the user

5. Checking the backup base (Full & then Diff/Tlog)

6. Checking if the job is disabled

7. Checking if the steps in job has failed

8. Checking if the job owner has changed

SQL server stopped

When the SQL server is stopped, it can be diagnosed and resolved by:

1. Pinging the server and checking the status

2. Checking whether the services are running well

3. Making sure the TCP end points are configured properly.

4. Checking the firewall settings.

5. Checking the authentication & user privileges.

6. Restarting the instance after confirming the Trace Flags

7. Check the information in Event viewer to see what has caused the DB Server down.

Queries running slowly

When the queries are running slowly, it can be diagnosed and resolved by:

1. Checking if the issue is with network communication.

2. Checking if there is adequate memory in the server computer and also enough memory available for DB Server.

3. Checking disk activity

4. Checking and analyzing the cache utilization

155

5. Checking if there are any issues like Locking/Blocking/Deadlock

6. Checking if the indexes are created or not

7. Verifying the I/O of the query

8. Verify scan density using the commands as per database. For example: DBCC SHOWCONTIG or DBCC UPDATE_STATISTICS for SQL server

Common incidents in webservers

Webserver stopped

When the webserver is stopped, it can be diagnosed and resolved by:

1. Check if there are any memory issues?

2. Restart or reload the webserver

3. Check the logs and enabling verbose logs

4. Check the syntax of the configuration files

5. Check the virtual host definitions

6. Check if there are any conflicting directives

Webserver doesn't start

When the webserver doesn't start, it can be diagnosed and resolved by:

1. Checking the SSL certificates and SSL session cache

2. Checking if there is any blocking ports

3. Checking if there is any conflicting software

4. Checking the configuration files, and determine if there is any missing or corrupted or improperly named files.

5. Checking the full error log

Webserver running slowly

When the webserver is running slowly, it can be diagnosed and resolved by:

1. Checking if there is any problem with the network? By pinging and ensure that you aren't losing any packets. Also try doing a 'traceroute' to make sure nothing in between the systems is causing trouble.

2. Checking what kind of webpages are slow? static, php, etc.?

3. Checking the log files? like error log or any other scripting language's that is being used.

4. Checking how much RAM is on the system?

5. Checking if there were any recent changes, check if there were any firewall changes?

6. Checking if there were any updates of database, scripting language?

7. Checking if there are any changes on database settings, table structures? Constraints? Procedures?

8. Checking if everything is fine from webserver, then check if there are any issues with the database to see if there are any locks that your application is waiting for?

Recap on your understanding

Understanding the curiosity and aspirations of people for IM profiles, here are a few interview questions that can be helpful for aspiring IM professionals as mentioned below:

- What is an incident?

- What is the purpose of incident management?

- What is ITIL? What are the phases of ITIL lifecycle?

- In which lifecycle phase does incident management fall into?

- What are the other processes in Service operations?

- What is the difference between an incident and problem?

- What is the difference between an incident and major incident?

- What is the difference between an incident and event?

- What is the process flow for incident management?

- What is the difference between SLA and OLA?

- What is a process and function?

- What is impact, urgency, and priority?

- What does RACI stand for? What is the purpose of RACI matrix?

- What is a KEDB and known error?

159

- What is the difference between a service request and an incident?

Interview questions for incident management profiles

How can I define a categorization structure for incident tickets?

Every ITSM stakeholder is very much familiar with the CTI (Category, Type, and Item) classification structure; hence, I would be discussing more in detail how you can segregate your incidents. Here is the list how you can segregate your incidents, for example:

Category: Hardware incidents (with respect to IT), Software incidents (with respect to IT), Facilities incident.

Subcategory/ Type: Computer, Network, Storage, Voice, Application, Database, etc.

Item: Hardware error, Hardware malfunctioning, Software error, Network connectivity error, Network device malfunctioning, Data or file corrupted or missing, Storage limit exceeded, Release failed, Missing or stolen, System or application hangs, Authorization error, Login failure, Virus alert

More detailed view on incidents categories

Hardware incidents can be classified as
Servers
Client systems

161

Mainframe
Laptop
Desktop
PDA's
Printing and scan devices
Networking devices

Software incidents can be classified as
Operating system
Virtual operating system
Virtual computer
Web software
Database
Applications

Facilities Incident can be classified as
Power systems
Temperature maintenance systems
Fire accidents
Water accidents

You may also include another classification as "cause" representing availability issues, security issues, performance issues, etc.

How to prioritize incidents?

Prioritizing incidents can be done by defining impact and urgency which will be done based on the SLAs signed with customers. Here is my opinion how you can define impact, urgency, and priority codes:

Impact	Affected users
1	More than 100 users
2	More than 50 users
3	More than 10 users
4	1-2 users

Urgency	To be resolved in
1	Less than 30 minutes
2	Less than 1 hour
3	Less than 3 hours
4	Less than 2 days

Priority	Code

1	Critical
2	High
3	Average
4	Low

And priority can be calculated by the formula: P= (Impact + Urgency)/2

Imagine the impact of an issue is 1 with reference to the above chart and urgency is 1, then the priority will be 1.

Imagine the impact of an issue is 3 and urgency is 2, then the priority will be 2.

Common issues in Incident management, which creates discrepancies?

- Mismatch between categorization of incidents in SD tools and IM tools.

- Mismatch between prioritization calculations in SD tools and IM tools.

- Lack of communication or proper interlock meetings between problem management staff and process owners.

- Inappropriately defined or lack of RACI matrix.

- Unclear understanding on incident, major incident and problem.

- Usage of ambiguous classification in CTI like 'miscellaneous', 'others', 'unknown', etc.

- Both IM and SD managed by the same team, leading to overlooking the tasks.

- Different individual tools being used for different ITSM processes.

Can I close my incident ticket (to meet my SLAs) because I have created a problem record and handed it to PM team?

Ideally speaking, no you cannot close the IM ticket until the issue is resolved either by a temp fix/work around or perm fix.

Can I close my incident ticket when the PM team is identifying the root cause?

IM ticket can be closed only when the incident is resolved either by a temp fix or perm fix; the resolution can be a temp fix/work around or perm fix.

So if you have a temp fix provided by PM or if you know a temp fix for an issue (as a known error) and the services are restored, then yes you can close the incident ticket. And, a PM team can work to identify the root cause and discover the perm fix.

Can I close my incident ticket when the Change Management and Release and Deployment Management team are implementing and deploying the root cause?

Ideally speaking, no you cannot close the IM ticket until the issue is resolved.

What is the difference between incident management and DR?

Disaster recovery is a sub-process in risk management which defines procedures on how to cope with and continue the IT services (such as when a disaster occurs like a fire, flood, terrorist attack, etc.). Disaster can be defined as a breakdown of business services which has a very big impact on the entire organization.

Incident management is a process in ITSM which defines procedures on how to manage incidents in IT infrastructure. Incident management defines procedures for registering, categorizing, assigning, diagnosing, escalating, resolving, and closing an incident. An incident is defined as breakdown of IT services or reduction in the quality of IT services.

When do I have to create an incident record?

An incident record should be created for all major incidents and normal incidents which are new to the IM staff. The objective of creating an incident record is that it encapsulates all the information on an incident and will be useful for future references.

Assessing the impact of an incident is a big issue, and it cannot be done just based on EU's opinion?

Impact of an incident cannot be defined just based on EU's opinion. Hence, here is my advice:

Firstly, understand the impact by checking the SD ticket (which states end user's opinion).

Second, check the SLAs to understand the criticality of the service.

Third, check the CMDB to understand the associated services.

Finally, get in touch with the local IT staff (of that specific area where the incident occurred) to understand the impact of the incident.

Sometimes there are 3-7 major incidents at a point in time. As a major incident manager (MIM), is managing all of them is a very challenging task?

Multitasking on multiple major incidents is never a good idea even for a MIM; hence, assign each and every major incident to experienced and knowledgeable incident analysts or a major incident team. Share the procedures and technical expertise to every analyst (going to his desk) and keep doing the follow up's after every 5 minutes to ensure they are resolved and restored.

Tight SLAs is a big issue in my IM operations (we have 10 minutes to evaluate the priority, 30 minutes to make an action plan and update the customer, and 1 hour to restore the service).

IM operational staff always have a challenge to meet the SLAs, following the procedures, resolving them on time, and updating the customers requires great versatility.

Here the advice would be:

- Assess the incidents priority by using predefined priority calculations; hence, your organization should define appropriate priority calculators based on the SLAs defined.

- Use predefined templates for communicating with stakeholders (with respect to critical outage notifications, action plan on incident, incident impact analysis, etc.).

- Every IM analyst should just focus on one single incident at a given point of time (multi-tasking on different incidents can become very risky and costly).

I want to set up incident management process in my organization. Is there any prerequisite process or function that is a must for incident management?

As per ITIL v3, it would be good to have Service desk function as a prerequisite for defining IM.

My IM operations manages numerous customers. Can I manage all of the incidents (from different customers) in one single tool?

No, it cannot be done. If your company is providing 'IM as a service' for different customers, you got to have:

- different teams managing different customers

- explicit ITSM tools for managing their incident information

- explicit SLAs with respect to each customer

Should all P1 incidents be treated as Major incidents?

No, P1 incidents cannot be called major incidents.

P1 actually signifies the priority of an incident which is determined by the priority calculators or assessments done on impact and urgency.

And major incidents are those incidents which disrupts the business critical services impacting a very huge number of users. Major incidents are very close to disasters and they will be dealt with special procedures and a special team would be dealing major incidents.

Who should decide if an incident is a major incident or not?

Major incidents are those incidents which impact huge number of users and will break continuity of services.

Hence, major incidents criteria should be clearly defined by the customers like:

- If an incident impacts more than 2000 end users of an organization.

- If there is an incident which breaks the internet service, during business hours impacting different business departments.

Is it okay to pause or stop the SLA clock on an incident?

No, it's never advisable to pause or stop the SLA clock for an incident.

Can a major incident be treated as a problem?

No, it cannot be treated as a problem. Please refer to the definition of a problem.

Is it necessary to conduct Major Incident Review (MIR)?

Yes, it is a must to conduct MIR as MIR captures all the important details about the major incident like:

- What caused the incident?

- How was the incident resolved?

- Who resolved it?

- Did we meet the SLAs?

- How can we prevent recurrence of the failure?

- What were the discrepancies that happened while restoring the MI? And how can we do it better next time?

- What were the positive things that happened while restoring the MI?

Is there any approach or procedure for preparing a major incident report?

A major incident report should encapsulate all information about the major incident right from the inception to the closure phase.

Firstly, define in policies that a specific role (major incident manager/major incident analysts) has to prepare the major incident report after every major incident closure.

Secondly, define in policies to conduct a meeting (involve all IM staff and major incident management team), to discuss the holistic details on every major incident (to investigate the issue), and to identify who will consolidate the information.

Thirdly, the designated person will collect information from all sources like event management tools (what events were triggered before the incident happened), how was the impact analyzed, who all have participated in resolving the incident, what troubleshooting procedures were executed, when was the incident restored, did we meet the SLAs, what were the mistakes performed while restoring the services, and what was the impact for services.

Fourth, prepare the report and send it to the Incident manager and the Major incident manager.

Fifth, document the lessons learned in KB and update them in CMS.

Finally, if there are any recommendations or feedback, update them in the CSI register.

Can an incident become a problem?

No; we should understand that an incident is a breakdown of a service or reduction in the quality of IT service, offered by the service provider. And a problem is the root cause of an incident or more incidents.

So, an incident can never become a problem.

What are the skills needed for Major Incident Manager?

Please check the section "Roles and responsibilities for Major Incident Manager"

Who all should be involved in making decisions on major incidents?

Key stakeholders needed for discussing issues on major incidents are:

Major incident manager, Service delivery manager, Incident manager, Technical management team, and Service owner.

Can I have two different IM tools for managing the IM operations in my IT?

Ideally speaking, it's advisable to have only one IM tool being used for all IM operations.

But assuming your IM operations are happening at two different locations, one in Europe and another in China. And if the management wants to use their own preferred tools, in such situations, it is okay to have two different tools.

Another instance would be an application support team using a tool for managing the application related issues. And a service desk/IM team using a specific tool for logging the service desk interactions and incidents.

Can I have two or more IM processes (one for application support and one for service desk) in an organization?

No, you cannot define two or more IM processes in one IT organization. You should have one standard IM process for all IT operations.

What is the difference between business continuity management and incident management?

Business continuity management defines the procedures for continuous risk analysis and management in organizations operations, through and after an outage or disruption (which generally involves natural disasters, terrorism attacks, and also technological issues.

Incident management defines the procedures for restoring the services as soon as possible.

Who all should be involved in major incident bridge call?

Major incident manager,

Problem manager,

Change manager,

SLA manager,

Relevant technical SME's.

In your opinion, what all can be done in order to reduce the number of incidents?

Provide a self help tool with frequently occurring issues, so that users will check the frequently occurring issues in self help tool before logging an incident.

Identify the recurring issues or incidents and identify the permanent fixes logging as problem tickets.

Have a streamlined change management and release management, doing meticulous planning and good risk assessment

Implement monitoring tools and do good monitoring

In your opinion, what databases should be accessible to incident management staff?

CMDB

Knowledge base or SKMS

How would you bring the right subject matter experts to ensure the efficient and timely resolution of any IT incidents?

By identifying the affected CI, and the categorization of the incident (category, type and item), it would be ideal to bring the respective technical SME's.

How would you ensure there is continuous improvement on incident management?

By checking the weekly and monthly trends, to understand the previous Csat, Quality rating/ scores, SLA adherence.

By giving regular trainings to IM staff

By daily review on the metrics and KPI's

By asking the IM staff to identify improvement opportunities

By regular personal talks with IM staff to understand the issues happening day to day.

What kind of data will you present in your incident management reports for top level management, mid level management, and operational management?

Incident management reports will vary for top level, middle level and operational management.

Very detailed information like number of incidents per day/ week/ month, time taken to resolve the incident, Csat (positive and negative), SLA adherence, number of tickets SLA breached, Quality adherence, Reason for breaching the SLA, number of incidents reopened, number of wrong assignments, number of incidents closed per week, etc. is reported for the operational management.

Comprehensive information like number of incidents per week/ month, Csat, SLA adherence, Quality adherence, SLA credits & penalizations, etc is reported for mid level management.

Brief and very important information like total number of incidents per month, Csat, SLA adherence, SLA credits and penalizations is reported to top level management.

How would you ensure there is complete ownership of the incidents lifecycle?

By checking how many incidents have been resolved every day.

By checking how many incidents are in pending status and their reason.

By checking how many incidents have been reopened and the reason.

By doing regular follow ups to see which incidents are about to breach the SLA's

As an incident manager, what would you do to increase the number of knowledge articles in knowledge base?

Identify the issues where there are no reference materials/ knowledge articles and accordingly request the problem management/ technical management/ knowledge management teams to create more number of articles.

What is your opinion on reopening a closed incident?

Generally once the incident is resolved, and after 3-4 days the incident ticket is closed.

So reopening the closed ticket is not a good parameter with respect to metrics. But if the IM policy says that you can reopen the incident ticket even after closing the ticket, we will have to follow it.

Or else the other approach is logging a new incident.

As per your experience, what should be done with the incident, when a RFC is logged?

Closing incidents after logging a RFC is not a good idea, as the customer will not be happy if the incident is closed.

Yes, if the incident is associated with a RFC; its definitely going to impact the metrics and SLA's. Hence you can set a status for the incident like "Pending due to a change" and ensure that the metrics are not impacted.

What would you do with an incident, where the customer/ end user is not responding to you for closing the incident?

If the users are not responding to the IM staff email/ phone calls, they can follow "3 strikes "policy.

This policy is about contacting the user 3 different times on 3 consecutive days; and failure to make contact with the user would lead to closure of the incident.

How would you automate the confirmation of users to close the incident or reopen the incident?

Notification templates can be designed in ITSM tools which will sent to the user when the incident ticket is set to

"Resolved" status. These notifications would ask for user's response whether:

if the incident is resolved and if it can be closed - Yes

if the incident is still existing and its needs to fix – No

If the user selects yes, then the ticket will be automatically closed. If the user selects no, then the ticket will be reopened.

Would you consider closing the major incidents after the issue is resolved or keeping it open for a couple of days to monitor the status?

Major incidents should be closed once the issue is resolved and a confirmation is obtained from the end users as it enables to capture the accurate metrics and simplifies the management of the IT operations (as major incident creates great attention to all IT stakeholders).

Would you raise a major incident if it was for a very short span of time?

Yes, if the incident serves the defined major incident criterion. We will have to raise a major incident ticket.

Imagine if there was an incident which was for half a second or a second, then the impact of that issue wouldn't be so high. Hence that cannot be raised as a major incident, but the events can be investigated to identify the root cause and prevent further recurrences.

Appendix

Acronyms

BIA – Business Impact Analysis

CI – Configuration Item

CMDB – Configuration Management Database

CMS – Configuration Management System

CSAT – Customer Satisfaction

CSF – Critical Success Factors

CSI – Continual Service Improvement

DFSS – Design for Six Sigma

DMAIC – Define, Measure, Analyze, Improve and Control

DMADV – Define, Measure, Analyze, Design and Validate

EM – Event Monitoring

KPI – Key Performance Indicators

ITSM – Information Technology Service Management

RACI – Roles, Accountability, Consulted, and Informed

RCA – Root Cause Analysis

IMIS – Incident Management Information System

IM – Incident Management

MTBF – Mean time between failures

MTBSI – Mean time between system incidents

MTO – Maximum tolerable outage

MTRS – Mean time to restore service

MTTR – Mean time to repair

ND – Natural Disaster

OLA – Operational Level Agreement

PM – Problem Management

SACM – Service Asset and Configuration Management

SLA – Service Level Agreement

SLM – Service Level Management

SOP – Standard Operating Procedures

SPOC – Single Point of Contact

KB – Knowledge Base

KEDB – Known Error Database

UC – Underpinning Contracts

VBF – Vital Business Function

Index

Printed in Great Britain
by Amazon

55304157R00106